Finding Yourself in Transition

Also by Robert Brumet

The Quest for Wholeness: Healing Ourselves, Healing Our World

Life Transitions: Growing Through Change (audiocassette)

Finding Yourself in Transition

Using Life's Changes for Spiritual Awakening

ROBERT BRUMET

UNITY® Books

Unity Village, Missouri

Unity Books is part of Unity House, a publishing imprint of Unity School of Christianity.

To receive a catalog of all Unity publications (books, cassettes, compact discs, and magazines) or to place an order, call the Customer Service Department: 1-800-669-0282.

Fifth printing June 2003

Cover design by Chad Pio.
This original artwork is an adaptation of the early sixteenth-century woodcut *The Vision of Ezekiel.*

The Revised Standard Version used for all Bible verses, unless otherwise stated.

LIBRARY OF CONGRESS CATALOGING-IN-PUBLICATION DATA
Brumet, Robert.
    Finding Yourself in Transition / Robert Brumet. — 1st ed.
        p.   cm.
    Includes bibliographical references.
    1. Change—Religious aspects—Christianity. 2. Life change events—Religious aspects—Christianity. 3. Spirituality—Unity School of Christianity.   I. Title.
BV4908.5.B75   1995
248.4'8997—dc20   94-17226
ISBN 0-87159-272-X (pbk.)   : $12.95
Canada BN 13252 9033 RT

Dedication

This book is dedicated to my children and to my children's children: Brenda, Steve, Eric, Andrea, Steven, Eric, Stephanie, and Alisha.

Acknowledgments

I owe a great deal to William Bridges, author of the book *Transitions*. I am indebted as well to many other authors and teachers that have guided and influenced my journey thus far. A partial list would include: Shinzen Young, Sandra and Garth Matthes, Carl Jung, Stephen Levine, Joseph Campbell, Pierre Teilhard de Chardin, Robert Bly, Kahlil Gibran, G. I. Gurdjieff, Werner Erhard, Ram Dass, Matthew Fox, Barbara Marx Hubbard, and my teachers of Native American spirituality.

I also owe much to the many friends and family members who have given me support and encouragement throughout this writing project. I love each of you.

Table of
Contents

Foreword

Perhaps we would agree that the keynote of life is change. We see it everywhere present in nature: the tadpole becomes a frog, the larva of the Monarch butterfly becomes an exquisite winged creature. Change is especially evident in the trees. When the air chills, the leaves change color and shower down, leaving the trees dark and bare. And then, as winter moves into spring, once again the trees come alive, first with a new ghost of green and then bursting forth with a rich collage of foliage. The whole universe is woven with a harmonious ebb and flow.

And, just as there is a harmonious ebb and flow in nature, there is also a divine rhythm at work in our individual lives. The patterns of our days are marked by endings and new beginnings. Every one of us is an integral part of the cosmic dance of the universe.

Although we understand intellectually that there are natural transitions at work in the universe, when change comes rapidly in our individual lives, we may question the meaning and purpose in what we are experiencing.

This is why I'm so excited about Robert Brumet's book *Finding Yourself in Transition*. Reverend Brumet, with his gentle wisdom and clarity of thought, shows us ways to move courageously and victoriously through the necessary but often unsettling transitions that are a part of our growth and development.

Robert is a longtime friend and colleague; I know many of his own transitions which have provided the impetus for this book. Although he writes from his own experience, he also draws upon the experiences and teachings of others. Certainly, in a world that is changing so rapidly and with so many people in transition, this book may well become a handbook for those who are experiencing turning points in their lives.

When my grandparents, Charles and Myrtle Fillmore, began Unity, they desired to establish a school of what they called "practical Christianity." In their search for Truth, they explored many philosophies and religions to develop what has become the Unity way of life.

Robert Brumet follows the same spirit of practical spirituality. Drawing upon many sources, Reverend Brumet masterfully weaves together strands of psychology, Eastern and Western mysticism, Bible interpretation, and personal history to bring us a new version of contemporary, practical spirituality.

Finding Yourself in Transition helps us discover the deeper meaning in the disturbing, unsettling events that happen in our individual lives and in the world. This book also reminds us that we are never alone, that the loving Intelligence that created us and all of life is ever present, guiding and directing our ways.

One of my favorite Bible quotations is from the third chapter of Ecclesiastes: "For everything there is a season and a time for every matter under heaven." And there is the natural flow of seasons in our own lives. We experience seasons of activity and growth and seasons of rest and renewal. Life is about growth, unfoldment, and change, which give us the incentive to explore new dimensions of living.

I hope, dear readers, that you will find this book as helpful as I have. God bless you on your journey.

Rosemary Fillmore Rhea
Prairie Village, Kansas
January 1994

Preface

Several years ago I dreamed that I was living in this particular house. It was the house of my childhood, the house in which I lived for sixteen years. In this dream, my wife and I and our four children were inside the house enjoying one another's company. Suddenly, the house began to shake. The walls began to cave in; the ceiling started to fall. In panic, I shouted, "Everyone, get out quickly!" I ran out the front door as fast as I could. The ground beneath my feet was shaking violently. I turned to look behind me, and as I did, I saw the house collapse into a pile of rubble. Everyone inside was killed; everything in it was destroyed. I was shaken to the very depths of my being.

And then, I looked up at the night sky and saw millions of crystal stars looking down upon me. Suddenly, I felt at one with all that my eyes could see. In that instant, I experienced, simultaneously, bottomless grief and infinite joy. I then knew that these were but opposite sides of the same coin. I sensed the death of my old life and the birth of a new one. This was the beginning of my transition.

Three years later my twenty-five-year marriage had come to an end. My work as minister of a Unity church was over. My life was in chaos. I was nearly bankrupt. My sense of identity was demolished. The pain and confusion felt overwhelming. I stood, in shock, looking at the rubble that was once my life.

At age forty-five, I felt as if my life was over.

It was. The new life that has emerged is not the same as the old one. Out of the ashes of the former life, a new birth has taken place. Indeed, God *was* in charge—yet in the midst of my darkness, I could not see that. I had no maps, no guidelines, no history upon which I could draw in order to understand my experience.

I have since encountered many other persons struggling with the pain and uncertainty of transition. I saw that they, like myself, were totally unprepared for the impact that change would have on their lives. I realized that our culture—in spite of the enormous changes that have occurred since the mid-sixties—offers us little in the way of help in coping with change. The world of my youth was a world where change was simply not acknowledged. And if the change was so great that it *must* be acknowledged, then it was treated as a tragedy from which we must recover as quickly as possible so that we could return our lives to "normal." Such was the only model for change that I knew.

Even though the world of today bears little resemblance to the world of my youth, I see and hear individuals responding to change much in the same manner that I was taught: Ignore the past and "get on" with life! The problem with this approach is that it doesn't work! Yet we seem to keep trying— perhaps because we don't know any other way. Perhaps it's time to find another way!

This book has two objectives. One is to offer an

alternative model for navigating one's way through life's transitions—to provide somewhat of a "map" for the journey. A second, and perhaps more important objective, is to help the reader discover that a major life transition is an opportunity for transformation—a transformation into an entirely new life. A transition is an opportunity for spiritual rebirth if we see clearly and respond wisely. I hope that this book will serve as a guide to that end.

This book is divided into three major sections. The first discusses the general nature of change and the dynamics of the transition process. The second section looks at the individual components of the transition process and parallels each with the biblical story of the Exodus, the journey of the Israelites from their bondage in Egypt into the Promised Land of Canaan. The third section looks at transition from a broader philosophical perspective and addresses questions such as: What's it all about? Where is this taking us? Does it ever end?

Note to Teachers

This book is amenable for use as a text in teaching a course in life transitions. The chapter summaries are designed to aid the instructor in presenting a class or workshop from this material. If time is limited, Chapters 5, 7, 9, or 10 could be summarized or eliminated without impairing the basic thesis of the text. The students should, however, be encouraged to read these chapters since they greatly enrich the more basic material.

A Note on Gender

I, like every writer of this decade, have struggled with the issue of gender when using pronouns such as "she/he" or "him/her." When it does not damage the integrity or the readability of the text, I try to balance the use of gender reference. In this book, however, there are instances when the individual referenced is traditionally or archetypally male. Please know that my use of the pronoun "he" in these cases does not signify an insensitivity to this issue of inclusiveness.

Prologue

Allons! whoever you are come travel with me!
Traveling with me you find what never tires.

The earth never tires,
The earth is rude, silent, incomprehensible at first,
      Nature is rude and incomprehensible at first,
Be not discouraged, keep on, there are divine
      things well envelop'd,
I swear to you there are divine things more beauti-
      ful than words can tell.

Allons! we must not stop here,
However sweet these laid-up stores, however con-
      venient this dwelling we cannot remain here,
However shelter'd this port and however calm
      these waters we must not anchor here,
However welcome the hospitality that surrounds
      us we are permitted to receive it but a little
      while....

Listen! I will be honest with you,
I do not offer the old smooth prizes, but offer
      rough new prizes,
These are the days that must happen to you:
You shall not heap up what is call'd riches,
You shall scatter with lavish hand all that you earn
      or achieve,

You but arrive at the city to which you were des-
tin'd, you hardly settle yourself to satisfaction
before you are call'd by an irresistible call to
depart,
You shall be treated to the ironical smiles and
mockings of those who remain behind you,
What beckonings of love you receive you shall only
answer with passionate kisses of parting,
You shall not allow the hold of those who spread
their reach'd hands toward you....

Allons! to that which is endless as it was beginning-
less,
To undergo much, tramps of days, rests of nights,
To merge all in the travel they tend to, and the
days and nights they tend to,
Again to merge them in the start of superior journeys,
To see nothing anywhere but what you may reach
it and pass it,
To conceive no time, however distant, but what
you may reach it and pass it,
To look up or down no road but it stretches and
waits for you, however long but it stretches
and waits for you,
To see no being, not God's or any, but you also go
thither,
To see no possession but you may possess it, enjoying all without labor or purchase, abstracting
the feast yet not abstracting one particle of it,

To take the best of the farmer's farm and the rich
   man's elegant villa, and the chaste blessings
   of the well-married couple, and the fruits of
   orchards and flowers of gardens,
To take to your use out of the compact cities as
   you pass through,
To carry buildings and streets with you afterward
   wherever you go,
To gather the minds of men out of their brains as
   you encounter them, to gather the love out
   of their hearts,
To take your lovers on the road with you, for all
   that you leave them behind you,
To know the universe itself as a road, as many
   roads, as roads for traveling souls.
                                    —Walt Whitman[1]

Part I

The
Paradox of Change

"The moment of change is the only poem."
—Adrienne Rich[1]

They sat in a circle. Each person shared his or her feelings: "I feel as if the bottom has dropped out of my life." "I don't even know who I am anymore." "My life is changing so fast that my head is spinning." "I feel so alone ... so alienated." The sharing continued with each person voicing rather similar feelings. Each person was in transition.

This particular group was formed to support individuals caught in the throes of change. There are hundreds, perhaps thousands, of similar groups across the country and around the world. Each group is intended to help individuals deal with the personal impact of change.

In this present age of uncertainty, perhaps the only thing certain is that life will change. Change is an inevitable part of our human experience. This has been true for humans in every era and is especially true for us who live near the start of the twenty-first century. Most of us who live today are witnessing and experiencing more changes in a few years than our ancestors would likely have experienced in the course of a lifetime. These changes continue to occur at an ever-increasing rate. Indeed, it appears as if time itself has somehow speeded up.

Rapid changes are occurring not only in the world around us but also in the world *within* us. These changes are not just in technology or lifestyle but are radical changes in the way that we perceive ourselves and our universe. Such changes are not just about how we live but about who we are as human beings. Our assumptions about who we are and how we are related to the world around us are being challenged, if not shattered.

These days we hear references to a "paradigm shift" that is occurring in our culture. The word *paradigm* is derived from the Greek word *paradeigma*, meaning "pattern." A pattern is a model or a guide used for making something. A paradigm is the underlying and largely unconscious set of assumptions that we use to interpret the meaning of a particular observation or experience. We have paradigms that govern how we see and understand the universe around us. We have paradigms that govern how we see ourselves and our relationship to the universe. When our earth was discovered to be round, not flat, everyone had to rethink our understanding of almost everything. When a paradigm shifts, we not only see and understand new information, but the very way in which we see and understand is altered. Such is the magnitude of change that is occurring.[2]

Despite the mind-boggling depth and swiftness of change in recent years, very few of us in this culture have learned to deal with change in a healthy way. We often fear and resist change. Our resistance is often subtle and unconscious. It would seem that despite our conscious intentions, there is a part of us that stubbornly clings to the old and the familiar. Some of us have consciously chosen to embark upon a journey of personal growth and transformation, ostensibly seeking and welcoming change. We may have affirmed: *I am willing to be changed,* and yet, ironically, there is something within us that unconsciously resists these very changes that we consciously desire. We may be puzzled to find ourselves resisting change as if our lives were at stake! For some reason, it seems that the greatest of all human fears is fear of the unknown, and change, especially deep or sudden change, almost always confronts us with the unknown.

Perhaps the deepest of all human needs is the need to find meaning in our experiences. Dr. Viktor Frankl maintains that the fundamental human drive is this quest for meaning.[3] For example, the child whose parents are divorcing, the woman who hears that she has cancer, the investor who learns that the stock market has just crashed will each wonder what this means. Not only will they seek meaning, but this desire is so strong that they may automatically, and unconsciously, ascribe a certain meaning to the event. It is not so much the event itself that will alter our lives as much as the meaning we give to it.

Counselors and ministers who work with people experiencing loss or tragedy in their lives will often hear questions such as: Why did this happen? What is the meaning of this event? In these challenging times, meaning is of crucial importance. It seems that when there is meaning, we can endure almost anything. The philosopher Nietzsche has said, "He who has a *why* to live for can bear almost any *how*."[4] Without meaning, it could seem that any such experience is unbearable.

Change, especially deep or sudden and unexpected change, challenges and perhaps even shatters the meaning and the understanding that we have created to "make sense out of life." We have developed our meanings as "road maps of reality" to guide us through the journey of life. They are part of the paradigm which patterns our perceptions and understanding. Change often takes us into new territory where old maps are no longer sufficient.

Theologian Paul Tillich makes reference to an ontological crisis which is a condition that arises when something that has served as the "ground of being" has been threatened, diminished, or taken from our life. This ground of being might be a social role, a relationship, an internal identity, or a belief system. The triggering event could be the death of a parent or a child, a divorce, a serious illness, a financial disaster, or any of several unexpected events. To many, such an experience feels almost worse than death itself.

Indeed, every change *is* a type of death, a death to an old way of living or being. Yet, ironically, change—a dying to the old—is one of the defining characteristics of growth. To live is to grow; to grow is to change; to change is to die to the old. Jesus of Nazareth said to his disciples, "Unless a grain of wheat falls into the earth and dies, it remains alone; but if it dies, it bears much fruit" (Jn. 12:24). The apostle Paul, who was no stranger to unexpected change, writes to the church at Corinth, "I die every day!" (1 Cor. 15:31) Many of us today are living in an accelerated pattern of growth and change and are, like Paul, "dying daily."

Yet we fear death, and this very fear of death, the fear of change, is also our fear of life itself. To be fully alive, we must be willing to be changed, to surrender into the moment without resistance; we must be willing to "die daily," even moment by moment. To resist these "deaths" is to resist life. To live fully is to realize that death—any type of death—is but a harbinger of new life. Thus we are ready to take the next step in our study of transition: our study of change, of death, and of rebirth into new life.

Chapter Summary

1. Change is inevitable. This has always been true but is especially so today.

2. Deep and radical changes are occurring around us and *within* us. Some of our basic assumptions about life are being challenged.

3. Few of us have learned to deal with change in a healthy way. We often resist change because it confronts us with our fear of the unknown.

4. One of the deepest human needs is the need for meaning. We use meaning as a "road map of reality."

5. Change often shatters our sense of meaning and takes us into new territory where the old "maps" no longer work.

6. Every change is a type of death. Yet, change is a characteristic of growth, and growth is a characteristic of life.

7. Our fear of death, of change, is fear of life itself. To resist death is to resist life, for every death is the harbinger of new life.

The
Process of Transition

Transition *is* a process. In our highly mechanized "quick-fix" culture, we generally don't
understand or appreciate the nature of process.
Those who lived in cultures more attuned to
nature understood and lived life as a process. The
processes of nature, such as the change of seasons,
the growth of crops, the migration of animals,
governed the lives of more primitive people. They
knew intimately the process of nature and the
nature of process. Their very survival depended
upon their ability to harmonize their lives with the
natural flow. Their spiritual lives, which were not
separated from their everyday lives, reflected their
deep appreciation for the wisdom and beauty of
the natural processes. We in our modern Western
culture are less attuned to the process of nature
than we are the clock and the calendar. We are
accustomed to planning and scheduling our lives
according to our own designs or the designs of
others rather than the processes of nature. Time
clocks, schedules, and deadlines govern the way
we live our lives. Relatively few of us eat when
we're hungry, sleep when we're tired, and wake

when we're rested. The clock, rather than the body, usually dictates the timing of these activities. The natural processes of our body, of our life, and of our environment are often ignored or overridden in favor of schedule or convenience.

Our mechanized world and consequent mechanistic life-style also influence the way we structure our self-image and even our sense of reality. We often talk about being "useful" and "productive," which is not necessarily bad, but we often equate our value as a person with usefulness and productivity. This attitude can lead us to see ourselves and others as machines to be used rather than as human beings to be loved and respected. We may unwittingly see ourselves as part of an economic machine that has in some ways become our master rather than our servant. A system which was designed to enrich our outer life may be contributing to the impoverishment of our inner life.

At one time the purpose of education was primarily for the personal growth of the individual. The word *education* is derived from the Latin word *educere* which means "to draw out." Education was intended to draw out the innate, unique wisdom of each individual. Today we tend to see education as primarily for the purpose of developing marketable skills and economic productivity rather than for self-development and the improvement of our quality of life. The "drawing out" of one's inner wisdom has been relinquished in favor of a process of "putting in" information and skills that seem to be needed to survive in our economic system. The needs of the individual have in many ways been usurped by the needs of the system. Our way of life has become largely based upon what could be called a "mechanistic paradigm."

Some time ago I bought a new car. It was a relatively simple procedure: I saw the car I wanted, negotiated a deal, traded in my old car, signed the legal papers, climbed into my new car, and drove away. On the way home, I thought, I wish all the changes in my life were this simple and direct! But they seldom are, and yet, how many of us, myself included, have tried to deal with our life changes in much the same mechanical way? How many of us are living in pain and confusion because we try to see all of our life transitions within this mechanistic paradigm?

Dealing with change in this mechanical way often results in pain and confusion because our inherent human nature is intrinsically related to natural processes. Our physical body functions as a process (or more accurately, as a set of processes). Our physical, psychological, and spiritual development also occurs as a process. A process is a change or a series of changes that occur over a period of time. A process usually has certain predetermined elements or phases that generally occur in a specific sequence or order. The phases or elements must each occur at the right time in the right order.

Working effectively with any process requires

that we be willing to trust the divine wisdom and order inherent within the process. Trying to force our personal will on a process is usually counterproductive and may be very damaging. For example, trying to force a flower to blossom before it is ready may kill the flower. Attempting to make a child walk or talk prematurely may have a damaging effect on the child's psyche. Anytime we violate natural process, we do damage and often inflict suffering.

The mechanistic paradigm generally does not honor the divine order inherent within the natural process. Operating mechanically, we favor functionality, convenience, and predictability over trusting the wisdom of the process. Our mechanistic, consumerist life-style sees most things (and sometimes people) as here for our own use. This attitude has been damaging not only to our environment but also to ourselves, both body and soul. Perhaps the present ecological crisis is forcing us to change this attitude toward the environment and toward ourselves as well.

Indeed, there is a slow but growing awareness that we cannot continue on this same path of mechanicalness and unconsciousness toward our world and ourselves. We are attempting, perhaps haltingly, to change the way we relate to our natural environment. We are beginning to see our environment as an extension of ourselves rather than just another resource to be consumed. Similarly, a shift is gradually taking place in our attitude toward ourselves. Holistic healing, humanistic psychology, and creation spirituality[1] exemplify this shift. We are slowly moving toward a vision of humanity as being intrinsically related to nature and to the cosmos—a vision that honors ourselves and our environment as having inherent value that is absolute and unconditional.

Reflecting this vision, there is a trend toward handling our two greatest transitions, birth and death, in more conscious ways. There is growing sensitivity to the needs of the individuals undergoing these transitions—not only physical needs but their psychological and spiritual needs as well. A positive birth experience and subsequent positive bonding with the mother are being recognized as very important to the well-being of newborn children. Home and family-centered birthing are gradually replacing the former institutionalized birthing process. Likewise, the work of Dr. Elizabeth Kubler-Ross, the hospice movement, and many "conscious dying" projects, including the work of Stephen Levine, have all helped to honor and support many people in the transition of dying.

Perhaps it is time to bring this same awareness and sensitivity to other life transitions such as adolescence, marriage, mid-life changes, children leaving home, divorce, career changes, retirement, aging, and the many other transitions common to life in our culture. As we shall see later, this need has been recognized and dealt with in

certain other cultures. Perhaps our lack of conscious attention to the needs of individuals undergoing these transitions is one cause of the psychological and spiritual malaise that permeates our
culture today.

Indeed, transition is a process. If we treat it
mechanically, then we may fail to learn from its
teaching and to gain the strength and wisdom
available from the experience, and we may unwittingly do damage to ourselves and others. To
understand the nature of the transition process
and to trust the divine order and wisdom inherent
within it provide us with the opportunity to use
transition as a time of accelerated growth and
learning. We shall explore this further in the next
chapter.

Chapter Summary

1. Transition is a process. More primal cultures were attuned to natural process. We in our culture are less attuned to the process of nature than to the clock and calendar.

2. Our mechanized world influences the way we see ourselves. We may see our value dependent upon our "usefulness." Our economic system has become our master rather than our servant. This is reflected in our educational system.

3. We live with a "mechanistic paradigm." We cause suffering when we try to handle transitions in a mechanical way.

4. A process is change occurring over a period of time. A process has certain elements that must occur in the right order and at the right time.

5. To work with a process, we must trust the divine order within it. To force our personal will upon a natural process is often damaging.

6. The mechanistic paradigm does not honor process; our desire for expedience and predictability often overrides natural process and causes us suffering.

7. There is a growing awareness that we cannot continue on this mechanical path. Our attitude toward the environment is shifting. We are starting to become more sensitive and aware in handling birth and death. Perhaps this attitude needs to be extended to other transitions.

8. Transition is a process; to understand its nature and to trust the wisdom within it allow us to use transition as a time for accelerated growth and learning.

Rites of Passage

One of my hobbies is canoeing. When canoeing, I sometimes encounter the phenomenon known as "white water." The water is white because it is running very swiftly, usually over submerged rocks. White water, to most canoeists, is both "good news and bad news." The bad news is that it is rather easy to capsize the canoe when in white water. And, if dumped in white water, one is more likely to be injured or even to drown. Also there is possible damage to the canoe and loss of contents. (Perhaps worst of all is the pain of embarrassment if seen by other canoeists!) So, the least desirable place to dump the canoe is in white water, yet this is the very time when that is most likely to happen.

And now for the good news: white water can be a lot of fun! It can be exciting and challenging, and one can make very rapid progress in white water. It is very interesting to note that the most dangerous part of the trip can also be the most rewarding.

Times of transition are like being in "white water." These can seem like difficult and dangerous times, and they can seem like exciting times when things move very swiftly. These can be times when we make very rapid progress in our spiritual growth.

A transition is often a time of crisis. We generally don't like the experience of crisis. We may not even like the sound of the word; however, the Chinese language presents us with an interesting perspective on the word *crisis.* In Chinese, the word *crisis* is formed by a combination of two other words: one word meaning "danger," the other "opportunity." One rather poetic translation I have heard refers to "crisis" as "opportunity riding on a dangerous wind." If we were to use the metaphor of sailing, rather than canoeing, we could see this same principle at work.

Transition may be an uncomfortable time, yet it is always a meaningful time. It is a time when the old order of our life is disrupted. It is a time when our old way of being is disturbed. It may even be a time when our sense of reality is challenged. Though painful, these can be extremely significant times in our life. Times of transition are wonderful opportunities to gain strength and wisdom—opportunities to experience spiritual breakthroughs and healings. Transition may provide the breakthrough necessary to live an entirely different life, not just the old life in a new way, but an entirely new life. Jean Houston writes:

> In times of suffering, when you feel abandoned, perhaps even annihilated,

there is occurring—at levels deeper than
your pain—the entry of the sacred, the
possibility of redemption. Wounding
opens the doors of our sensibility to a
larger reality, which is blocked to our
habituated and conditioned point of
view.... Pathos [suffering] gives us eyes
and ears to see and hear what our normal
eyes and ears cannot.[1]

And the poet Kahlil Gibran says, "Pain is the
breaking of the shell that encloses your understanding."[2]

Change, especially a major change or one that
intrudes swiftly and unexpectedly into our life,
often "breaks the shell" that encloses our understanding, even our sense of reality. Pain can show
us where we may be resisting the breaking of the
"old shell" and inhibiting the emergence of the
"larger reality," for indeed, most of our pain arises
from resistance. By understanding the dynamics of
the transition process, we can learn how to minimize our pain and facilitate the birth of the new
life.

Ray came to me because of a growing frustration with his work. He felt increasingly pressured.
He had frequent arguments with his boss and co-
workers. He felt stifled and unappreciated. This
frustration began to affect his health and family
life. He knew that he "needed a change," but he
didn't see any alternative for a "man his age

without a college degree." He felt trapped and confused. Ray was experiencing a great deal of pain.

Rather than keep looking for external answers, I encouraged Ray to observe his feelings, uncomfortable though they were. In learning to listen to his feelings, Ray gradually got in touch with their underlying message; he became aware of the deeper desires of his heart that were being frustrated by his current circumstance. Ray felt a strong need to be independent and creative. All of his life, he wanted to be in business for himself, yet circumstances never seemed to permit this. Further exploration found that Ray's deepest desire was to combine his favorite pastime, fishing, with his career goal. He began to explore this as a serious possibility.

Today Ray runs his own company, which manufactures fishing lures. He loves it immensely. It's a lot of work, but he "enjoys every minute of it." His wife and children have also become involved in the business. This has led to a whole new dimension in his family relationship. Ray may not be rich in an economic sense, but his life is much richer in many other ways. By listening to his pain rather than running from it, Ray was guided to a new life.

There are various kinds of transitions that we may encounter on our life journey. Some transitions are inevitable in our human experience, some are probable, and others are possible but perhaps not likely. Birth, adolescence, mid-life, old age, and death are transitions that virtually all humans experience, given an average life span. Graduation from school, marriage, job change, parenthood, and retirement are examples of transitions that the vast majority of us in our culture will experience. Divorce and career changes are transitions that were relatively rare fifty years ago yet are becoming increasingly commonplace today. Many, perhaps most of us, will never experience a debilitating accident or illness, a bankruptcy, or a job layoff.

Some transitions occur by choice and others are thrust upon us—ready or not! Some we can predict while others are rather unpredictable. Some transitions are pleasant and welcomed, others are unpleasant and usually unwelcomed. Certain transitions, such as retirement or divorce, may be welcomed by some and dreaded by others. Sometimes a particular transition may cause us considerable pain at its onset, yet in retrospect be seen as the turning point leading to a very positive life change.

Birth and death are our greatest transitions. In between, we experience innumerable others—wanted and unwanted, expected and unexpected, pleasant and painful—each different in its specific form, and yet each transition has some remarkably similar characteristics.

We will see that each transition consists of three rather distinct stages.[3] Each stage has its distinctive characteristics as well as its particular challenges and lessons to teach us. Each transition in general, and each stage in particular, has a specific gift for us if we but learn how to recognize and accept it.

First, each transition begins with an ending. Change means letting go of the old before we are able to embrace the new. So the first stage of the transition process is "Endings."

Many of us would like to believe that the stage of "Endings" is followed by a new beginning; it is not. The next stage is called "The Void." This stage is characterized by a feeling of emptiness and a sense of "wandering in the wilderness." Finally, we come to the last stage which is that of "New Beginnings."

One of the characteristics of process is that the phases or stages are not necessarily linear or clearly defined. The phases often overlap and sometimes seem to reappear after we "thought we worked through that one!" Although there is a theoretical point where we move from one stage to another, in real life, no such exact point in time exists. To use an analogy from the process of nature: we may say that winter ends and spring begins on March 21; although the general weather pattern may begin to change around this date, the day-to-day weather may vary markedly during this period. So it is with the stages of the transition process.

The three stages of the transition process—Endings, The Void, New Beginnings—parallel an ancient ritual known as a "rite of passage." A rite of passage consists of a ritual in which the initiate undergoes a symbolic death and rebirth—ending one phase of his or her life experience and beginning another.

Anthropologists have recognized that each rite of passage has three stages: a "separation" phase in which the initiate is removed from the old order and undergoes a symbolic death, an "initiation" phase in which the individual is then sent away from the tribe or village to confront and to experience the purpose and the meaning of his existence, and finally, a "return" phase in which the individual is reintegrated back into the social order as a totally new person.

Of all the rites of passage practiced by native peoples in various times and places, perhaps the most universal is the rite of passage marking the end of childhood and the beginning of adulthood, when the boy becomes the man; the girl becomes the woman. Typically, the individual is taken through some type of ritual that symbolizes the death of the child. In some cases, a funeral is actually staged. Often the child's name is taken away, eventually to be replaced by a new name; sometimes the child's parents will pretend to no longer see or hear him, for the child is dead and no longer exists.

Stripped of his identity, the initiate becomes a nonperson—invisible in the space between worlds. In this netherworld, he confronts his existence and is initiated into the world of the transpersonal. The initiate is empowered by a dream or a vision or a journey into the "other world." He receives a new name and a new identity, for he has died and is now reborn.

Returning to the tribe, the initiate now has a specific gift, a certain power to share with other people. He may become a hunter, a warrior, a shaman mandated to serve the greater good with his newly discovered power. He returns as a new person, a new being. The new self has emerged.

Although the term *initiation* is not specifically used in the Bible, there are many stories and teachings that allude to this process. Jesus had several experiences that have been referred to by some as "initiations." His going alone into the wilderness for forty days to be tempted by Satan is a classic illustration of a rite of passage. In Matthew 4:1, it is reported that "Jesus was led up by the Spirit into the wilderness to be tempted by the devil." From that experience, he emerged empowered to begin his public ministry "preaching the gospel of the kingdom" (Mt.4:23). Another very poignant example of a rite of passage is in the story of the crucifixion, burial, and Resurrection of Jesus. This is indeed the major event in his ministry, an experience from which he emerged with even greater powers than before.

The apostle Paul had his own experience of initiation which is sometimes referenced in his letters: "It is no longer I who live, but Christ who lives in me" (Gal. 2:20). He calls others to this same process: "Put off your old nature which belongs to your former manner of life ... and be renewed in the spirit of your minds, and put on the new nature, created after the likeness of God" (Eph. 4:22-24).

Even today some Christians who report to having had a certain transformative experience refer to themselves as "born again." Indeed, the motif of "dying to the old" and being "reborn" to a new life or a new level of consciousness is found in literature from virtually every age and culture.

The great mythologist Joseph Campbell speaks of the mythological hero, which is that person who, through an extraordinary resolve, is able to transcend the normal limitations of humankind and perform feats and deeds which appear superhuman. To quote a term from the *Star Trek* series, the hero is able to "go where no one has gone before." Campbell notes that every mythological adventure of the hero follows a path very similar to the initiate in his or her rite of passage:

> The standard path of the mythological adventure of the hero is a magnification of the formula represented in the rites of passage: *Separation—initiation—return.... A hero ventures forth from the world of common day into a region of supernatural wonder: fabulous forces are there encountered and a decisive victory is won: the hero comes back from this mysterious adventure with the power to bestow boons on his fellow man.*[4]

Each of us who is going through a transition is a potential hero, for we are leaving our old familiar world to venture into unmapped territory, not knowing what fate befalls us. Like the ancient mythological heroes, we will encounter the "dragons" of fear and self-doubt; we will engage fierce battles within our soul, and ultimately, we will, if we persist, discover "the treasure," the Holy Grail, the wonderful gift of freedom and power that each transition promises us if we but have the heart to take the journey. Let us begin.

Chapter Summary

1. A transition is like canoeing in white water—dangerous, yet exciting, an opportunity to make very rapid progress.

2. Transition is often a time of crisis. A crisis brings both danger and opportunity.

3. Transition may be uncomfortable yet is always meaningful. It's an opportunity for a breakthrough into a new life.

4. Pain is often a sign that a new level of understanding is breaking through. With right understanding, we can minimize our pain and allow the breakthrough to emerge.

5. We may experience many kinds of transitions in our life journey. Some are wanted, pleasant, expected, and some are unwanted and unexpected.

6. Each transition has three stages: "Endings," "The Void," and "New Beginnings."

7. These stages always occur in this order, yet there is often overlap and regression between the stages.

8. These three stages parallel an ancient ritual known as a rite of passage: a symbolic death and rebirth.

9. Each rite of passage has three stages: separation, initiation, and return.

10. A common rite of passage is one marking the end of childhood and the beginning of adulthood. The child

"dies" and is "reborn" into the adult world with a new identity and new power.

11. In the Bible, there are many personal experiences that could be considered a form of initiation.

12. The theme of dying to the old and being "born again" to a new life can be found in literature from virtually every age and culture—including our own.

13. Joseph Campbell identified the "mythical hero" who has transcended the normal limitations of humankind and may appear superhuman. Each of us in transition is a potential "hero."

Part
II

Endings

4

"What we call the beginning is often the end. And to make an end is to make a beginning. The end is where we start from."

—T. S. Eliot[1]

Everything in this phenomenal world has at least one thing in common: it all had a beginning, and it all will come to an end. The length of time, as we measure it, between beginning and end may be fractions of a second or millions of years, yet every form of physical life has a beginning and an end. Within the experience of a human lifetime, we have innumerable beginnings and endings. Every breath, every activity, every relationship has a beginning and an end. Our physical body had a beginning, and it will have an end. Each beginning is a type of birth, each ending a type of death.

We in the Western world are generally not comfortable with death in any form. We tend to acknowledge and celebrate beginnings and to deny and to lament endings. We rejoice at a birth yet often see death as a tragedy. We celebrate weddings but tend to see divorce as a failure. Even a graduation ceremony, an obvious time to acknowledge an ending, is referred to as a "commencement" and the keynote speaker will typically address "the vast and limitless future that lies ahead."

Certainly, there is much that is good and true contained within our social customs, yet often our conventional wisdom contains only half-truths. Good as it is that we celebrate beginnings, endings also need to be honored and perhaps even celebrated. We can truly experience a new beginning only when we have fully dealt with the ending that preceded it; otherwise, we simply carry the unfinished business of the past into the future.

Most of us do not handle endings very well. We have a tendency to either understate or overstate the importance of an ending. Let's look first at the understatement. The importance of an ending is understated when we fail to acknowledge the impact that it has on our lives, when we discount or minimize the effect it has on us. We may make statements such as "Let's forget about the past and 'get on' with life." Such a statement is valid within a certain context, but much of the time it is simply a cliché that we use to deny our true feelings about an ending.

One reason why we discount or minimize the importance of an ending is that it may be an attempt to manage the grief associated with a loss. Every ending is a loss, and grief is a normal response to loss. Grief is a painful emotion, and we instinctively try to protect ourselves from this pain. In addition, there may not be the emotional support needed from our family or friends to help us experience our grief. We may be admonished to "be strong" and to "stay in control." Except under rather restricted circumstances, our social customs generally don't support the experience of grief—especially with men.

As a result of our denial, many of us carry a reservoir of grief from previous losses in our life. Each ending may trigger this unresolved grief from the past as well as that from the current loss. If this seems too much to bear, we may attempt to avoid this pain with some form of denial or distraction. Tempting though it may be, this just adds to the "reservoir" and potentially creates more suffering. Consequently, we may become terrified of even a minor loss because of the "Pandora's box" that the next ending may open.

As we mentioned before, our culture has adopted somewhat of a "mechanistic" orientation toward life. This paradigm tends to see endings, especially unexpected endings, as a breakdown, as something "gone wrong." An unexpected ending may trigger our anxiety about the unpredictability of life. It may create a sense of being out of control and vulnerable to the apparent random events that impact and shape our lives. An unexpected ending does not fit into our vision of life functioning as a "well-oiled machine" that we personally operate.

To understate the importance of an ending is to discount its impact on our life, to not take it seriously enough. On the other hand, it is possible to take an ending too seriously, to overstate the impact that it has on our life. Two classic illustrations are with the lover who throws himself over a cliff when his sweetheart rejects him or with the millionaire who jumps off a bridge when his fortune is lost. There are other, less dramatic, ways that we may overstate the impact of an ending. Any time we see an ending as an absolute finality rather than the beginning of a transition process, we may be taking it too seriously.

Now, in one sense, every loss *is* permanent, otherwise, it would not be seen as a loss. To be sure, the person that died is gone permanently (in a physical sense); the relationship that ended probably *is* over for good; the lost circumstances of our life never will be exactly the same. However, what is *not* lost is the possibility of a new beginning. What is *not* lost permanently is our ability to live and to love and to enjoy life. In truth, as we accept endings as part of a greater life process, we ultimately increase our ability to live and love and enjoy life.

We shall see later that a certain sense of emptiness and meaninglessness accompanies many major life transitions. However, we overstate the importance of an ending when we perceive that this emptiness and meaninglessness is a permanent condition rather than the passage to a new life. We overstate the importance of an ending when we believe that the lost person, possession, or circumstance was that which gave our lives meaning and that without this outer condition our happiness is lost forever.

I often counsel my students to honor endings but not to worship them. To worship an ending is to give it more power than it deserves, to make it bigger than you are. To honor an ending is to acknowledge the impact that it has on our life; it is to honor the people and experiences that were important in our life; it is to honor the divine wisdom and order that govern every aspect of our life if we but have eyes to see it.

Now let's look at the various ways that we are impacted by an ending. William Bridges identifies "four different aspects of the natural ending experience: disengagement, disidentification, disenchantment, and disorientation."[2] We will look at each individually, yet they are all very closely related; in fact, it is common to experience more than one of them at a time. What follows is a description of each of these aspects of the ending experience.

Disengagement

One of the definitions of *engage* is to "interlock with" someone or something. To *disengage* is to "release" the interlocking that once existed. We usually become intricately "engaged" with the people, places, roles, and activities that are a regular part of our lives. The persons we see, the places we go, the activities and the social rituals in which we engage become an integral part of our everyday lives. We often don't realize just how intricate the interlocking is until we begin to disengage. Sometimes we fail to notice how important something is to us until it is no longer a part of our lives.

Endings often begin with a disengagement. The end of a marriage, a graduation, the loss of a job, all require us to disengage from what was once a familiar part of our lives. We may know that we are "beginning an ending" by changes in the external circumstances of our lives.

On the other hand, disengagement may not occur until "the end of an ending." For example, we may physically stay in a career or a relationship long after we have withdrawn our mental or emotional energies. The external ending may be the final step of an internal process that began months or even years ago.

It is usually difficult to ascertain exactly when or how an ending actually begins. And we can't always say exactly what the cause of an ending may be; causes exist on many different levels. The ultimate cause is always the one Presence and one Power we call God seeking to express through us more perfectly. It is essential that we listen to and trust this power at work in our lives in whatever form God is expressing, even if it feels painful or confusing at the time, for we rarely understand the reason for the changes in our lives when we are in the midst of our emotional reaction to them.

An ending separates us from the familiar elements of our life. In the traditional rites of passage, the initiation process requires the initiate to separate from his place in the social order. This is done by sending the person away from the village into the forest, cave, desert, or mountain to be alone. This external separation is symbolic of an internal separation that is taking place. The external separation is temporary; the internal separation is radical and permanent. The old life is released forever; something dies. The initiate will eventually return to the village but will never be the same person who left.

This pattern is portrayed in stories of the mythical hero, including many of those in the Bible. Jesus would venture off alone to pray when he was at a transition point in his life. His forty-day experience in the wilderness where he encountered "the devil" is an example of disengagement, as was his time alone in Gethsemane where he prepared himself for a major rite of passage at Calvary. Moses received the Ten Commandments from the Lord only after he disengaged from his tribe and went up to Mount Sinai alone. Elijah heard the "still small voice" of God while alone in a mountain cave during his forty days in the wilderness.

In our modern society, we have few formal rites of passage, yet we note that there is a strong tendency to break with the familiar social roles and patterns during times of transition; we often find ourselves wanting to be alone. We may unwittingly create a disengagement so that we can have the needed separateness. It is not uncommon for an individual to unconsciously "set up" the circumstances that force a disengagement. And we may at times find ourselves feeling "spacey" and seeming to live "in another world." This is the psyche's way of creating the internal space that we need to do our work in the "other world" of the soul.

Disidentification

Disengagement is primarily an external process; *disidentification* is an internal one. Much of our personal identity may be invested in the roles, activities, and relationships in which we are engaged. As such, we see ourselves reflected in those around us. When an ending shatters this outer mirror, it may feel as if a part of us is missing— sometimes a very large part. Much of the grief that we experience with an ending is the result of this loss of our connection to self. Alla Bozarth-Campbell writes:

> The more someone or something means to me, the more of myself I have invested, given over, or entrusted outside of myself. In being cut off from that some-one or something, I am in fact cut off from that part of me that the other represented. I have lost a part of my own self.[3]

One of the very strongest tendencies of a human being is to seek to maintain one's sense of identity. When we live with our identity on the outside, we will attempt to control our environment in order to protect this identity. We may go to great lengths to create and maintain the outer roles and structures that mirror to us the "self" that we want to see.

So powerful is this force to maintain our identity that many would die rather than let it go. One's identity is the center of gravity around which one seeks a sense of equilibrium. Just as the sun with the planets, our identity forms a field of attraction that determines the "orbit" of our thoughts, feelings, and behavior. Yet, when we are willing to let go of this cherished identity and to face our fear of the unknown, our fear of annihilation, and see beyond it, we enter into the experience of becoming who we really are, and who we really are already is more than we can ever imagine. Stephen Levine writes:

> In letting go of who we imagine ourselves to be, letting go of our thinking, our attempt to control the world, we come upon our natural being which has been waiting patiently all these years for us to come home.[4]

How do we let go of the "imagined self" and open up to our "natural being"? There may be many ways; much has been written about various paths to finding the true Self. Within the context of endings, Bozarth-Campbell tells us of a simple yet powerful way:

> Finding my way back to the missing part of myself, reclaiming it from the person or thing now gone, is the process I have called grieving. It is, literally, a life-saving process. Grieving is not only the way we survive a hurtful loss, but it is the way we can learn to live more creatively through and beyond the loss, into and out of a deeper part of ourselves.[5]

Grief is not just a symptom of being wounded but is a part of the very process by which we are healed. When we allow ourselves to grieve fully our loss rather than avoiding its lesson by seeking another external mirror, we are reclaiming the natural self. We are then like the prodigal son returning to the father after a long sojourn in the far country. Grieving our loss is a major step in coming home to our true Self.

Yes, we can get stuck in our grief; we can take our loss too seriously. Once again, the path of healing lies in honoring our grief as a rite of passage, something we move through in order to realize more fully who we truly are.

Jesus said, "Whoever loses his life for my sake will find it" (Mt. 16:25). Disidentification is a matter of losing one's former life, the life defined by externals, and having the opportunity to find one's true Self—the divine essence that is the Christ Spirit in each of us.

Disenchantment

To be "enchanted" is to live under a spell, and we all do; we are enchanted by our cultural paradigm. Every culture attempts to perpetuate its vision of reality through each of its members. Most of these collective beliefs are simply taken for granted, unconsciously assumed to be true by virtually everyone in the culture. We base our values, our ideals, our goals on these "self-evident truths" and are not even aware that we are embracing them until something causes us to challenge one of these assumptions.

For example, we may assume that external success brings happiness, a belief that has been one of our cultural standards. We may spend an enormous amount of time and energy accumulating material goods and social status, yet we're not happy. We may surmise that it's because we don't have "enough" or that it's not the "right kind," so we keep trying. Eventually, we *get it*! What we "get" is not "enough of the right stuff"; what we get is the realization that there's not enough "stuff" in the universe to make us happy. The very thing upon which we have based our life has suddenly vanished! Welcome to the land of *disenchantment*.

This example is but one of a myriad of enchantments that are spun by our culture.[6] These enchantments are not necessarily bad; they can serve us at a certain stage of our evolution, yet they can hinder us at other stages. What serves as a stepping-stone at one point in our journey may become a stumbling block at another. (Pity the adult who never believed in Santa Claus; pity more the adult who still does!) Much of our becoming an adult lies in giving up the enchantments of youth—but not too soon. Much of what we call spiritual growth is a process of stripping away our outgrown enchantments.

This all sounds like a very positive and desirable endeavor ... and it is; however, at the onset of disenchantment, it rarely seems so; in fact, it feels awful! Our sense of reality is challenged; our values are turned upside down; our purpose for living seems to disappear. Disenchantment is feeling as if the bottom has dropped out of our life.

Disenchantment differs from disappointment. Disappointment occurs when a particular person or event thwarts our desires or intentions. With disappointment, we don't question the underlying assumptions, we're simply upset that this one particular thing "didn't work." With disenchantment, we discover that the intention itself "doesn't work," that it rests on a fallacy. We could say that disappointment is when we discover that this man isn't the real Santa Claus; disenchantment is when we discover that there *is* no Santa Claus, and there never was.

Disenchantment may come after an external ending; a disengagement may be the trigger. It may also come before we experience any external change; the disenchantment itself may be the first sign of an ending. Such was the case with author Leo Tolstoy:

> At about the age of fifty, Tolstoy relates that he began to have moments of perplexity, of what he calls arrest, as if he knew not "how to live," or what to do.... Life had been enchanting, it was now flat sober, more than sober, dead. Things were meaningless whose meaning had always been self-evident. The questions "Why?" and "What next?" began to beset him more and more frequently....
>
> These questions "Why?" "Wherefore?" "What for?" found no response.
>
> "I felt," says Tolstoy, "that something had broken within me on which my life had always rested, that I had nothing left to hold on to, and that morally my life had stopped....
>
> "All this took place at a time when so far as all my outer circumstances went, I ought to have been completely happy. I had a good wife ... good children ... a large property ....
>
> "And yet I could give no reasonable

meaning to any actions of my life."[7]

Tolstoy's old life was coming to an end; a new life would eventually emerge and disenchantment was the first sign. His plight illustrates the confusion that often surrounds an ending. This confusion is part of another phenomenon of the ending experience: *disorientation*.

Disorientation

To be disoriented is to be "confused, to lose one's sense of direction, time, or perspective." An ending may trigger any or all of these experiences. One reason why this occurs is given by William Bridges:

> The "reality" that is left behind in any ending is not just a picture on the wall. It is a sense of which way is up and which way is down; it is a sense of which way is forward and which way is backward. It is, in short, a way of orienting oneself and of moving forward into the future.[8]

The "road maps" that we once used to guide our life may suddenly become useless. We may find that we are not only in "new territory" but that the "navigational instruments" we depended on no longer work; our entire sense of direction is disrupted. It's not just that we've lost our way; we've lost the sense of where we were going in the first place!

Our sense of past and future lies within the context of the set of meanings, values, and identities that comprise our reality. When these are shaken or shattered by an ending, our sense of past and future is likewise "scrambled." The continuity of our life may feel broken. This is referred to by Murray Stein as a state of *psychological liminality*:

> Liminality ... occurs: when the ego is separated from a fixed sense of who it is and has been, of where it comes from and its history, of where it is going and its future; when the ego floats through ambiguous spaces in a sense of unbounded time, through a territory of unclear boundaries and uncertain edges; when it is disidentified from the inner images that have formerly sustained it and given it a sense of purpose.[9]

Disorientation results from the dismantling of the old self, the old life, the old reality. It is a necessary step in the development of the new life, the transformed self, the greater reality.

Summary

We each carry within us a set of primary questions which have been formed early in our life. Normally, these questions are beneath the level of consciousness and are rarely verbalized. The answers that we've developed to these questions frame our sense of reality. The questions are:

Who am I?
What is real?
What is my life about?
What is my place in the world?

At a very young age, we begin to formulate answers to these questions. Our answers usually stay with us for a long time ... sometimes a lifetime. Nothing affects our life more than these answers. All of them are impacted by an ending.

Disengagement changes, or at least challenges, the beliefs we've formed about our place in the world—our roles, our relationships, our responsibilities. *Disidentification* shatters the way we answered "Who am I?" *Disenchantment* results from a break in our sense of "what is real." *Disorientation* occurs when our sense of "where my life is going" is disrupted.

Each of these aspects of the ending experience needs to be honored as an essential element of the transition process. There is no single "right way" to do this. It is important that we be aware of all our responses to an ending and allow ourselves to fully experience each stage of the process. As with any transformational process, we don't make it happen; we can only allow it to happen through us.

As we discussed earlier, this is often a time of crisis, a time of danger and opportunity, a time of breakdowns and breakthroughs. It is very important that we allow ourselves to have our feelings and our internal experiences and at the same time to be extremely cautious about making major decisions or long-term commitments. Our feelings and our perceptions may vary greatly from day to day. What seems so real and important today may seem trivial and irrelevant tomorrow. It may be a time to seek guidance and support from friends, support groups, and/or professional counselors.

It is especially important that we turn to the God of our understanding during these times of passage. Ironically, this is often a time when our faith in everything, including God, is shaken. Yet, if we can but realize it, the possibility for an entirely new understanding of God—and a new relationship with God—is emerging. Each transition allows us the opportunity for a "bigger God" than the one we once believed in. We can realize that God is not only guiding us through the transition but is the very force that is bringing about the transition—and the resultant transformation.

Chapter Summary

1. Everything in our visible world has a beginning and an end; each beginning is a birth, each ending a death.

2. We in the West are not comfortable with any form of death. We usually celebrate beginnings, but our endings also need to be acknowledged.

3. If we do not deal with our endings, we carry the unfinished business of the past into the future.

4. Most of us do not handle endings well; we often understate or overstate the importance of an ending.

5. We understate the importance of an ending when we fail to acknowledge the impact that it has on us.

6. We may discount the importance of an ending in an attempt to manage the grief from a loss.

7. We may carry inside us a reservoir of grief from previous losses. Each ending may trigger grief from previous losses as well as from current circumstances.

8. Living in a mechanistic paradigm, an unexpected ending may trigger our anxiety about the unpredictability of life.

9. To overstate the importance of an ending is to take it too seriously: to see it as an absolute finality rather than as the beginning of a transition process.

10. Although some conditions in life can be lost forever, we never lose the possibility for a new beginning, and we never lose the possibility for happiness. No outer cir-

cumstance is the real source of happiness.

11. Honor endings but don't "worship" them. Take them seriously, but never too seriously.

12. There are four aspects of the ending experience: disengagement, disidentification, disenchantment, and disorientation.

13. Disengagement means we are no longer engaged in what was once a familiar part of our life.

14. Disengagement is often, but not always, the beginning of the ending process.

15. We don't always know the cause of an ending; ultimately, it is God seeking to express more fully through us.

16. In traditional rites of passage, the process begins with separation from the social order. This theme is reflected in many biblical stories.

17. We don't have many formal rites of passage in our modern culture, and yet we may unconsciously create a separation experience.

18. Our outer world often mirrors parts of our identity; when we lose the outer "mirror," it may feel as if we have lost part of ourselves. This is disidentification.

19. One of our strongest drives is to maintain our sense of identity. If we are willing to face the fear of letting this go, we will begin to discover our true nature.

20. One of the ways we do this is by grieving our loss. We can find ourselves through our loss.

21. Every culture "enchants" its members through its system of collective beliefs and values. We usually assume these beliefs are true, without question. To be disenchanted is to have one of these basic assumptions shattered.

22. We may need these beliefs (i.e. enchantments) at certain stages of our growth, but at some point, we need to release them. Much of our growth consists of letting go of outgrown "enchantments."

23. Ultimately, this is a very positive thing, but it rarely seems so at the time; it usually feels awful!

24. Disappointment occurs when a certain circumstance fails to meet our desires, yet we continue with the same basic set of assumptions; disenchantment occurs when we drop the basic assumptions.

25. Disenchantment may come before or after a disengagement.

26. An ending may trigger disorientation: a sense of confusion, a loss of a sense of direction. The "maps" that we used to guide our life may suddenly become useless.

27. With disorientation, our sense of past and future is disrupted; the ego "floats" through a sense of unbounded time.

28. We unconsciously answer certain questions early in life. The answers influence our life enormously. The questions: "Who am I?" "What is real?" "What is my life about?" "What is my place in the world?" An ending impacts our answers to all of these.

29. There is no single "right way" to experience an ending. It is important to allow ourselves to have our feel-

ings and to be cautious in making major decisions.

30. At this time it is especially important to turn to the God of our understanding and to trust that we are being guided.

Departure From Egypt

Carl Gustav Jung, a Swiss psychologist, proposed the existence of an unconscious collective memory in the human psyche. Just as animals inherit instinctual knowledge common to the species, we humans, according to Dr. Jung, inherit unconscious memory patterns common to the human race. These memory patterns are known as archetypes.[1]

Archetypes could be thought of as "organs" of the mind. As each organ in the human body has a specific function that serves the well-being of the whole body, so each archetype in the collective unconscious serves the well-being of the whole psyche. Archetypal memories are not personal; they do not belong to the individual but to the human race. These memories can be accessed through dreams and visions and through the study of myths and ancient Scriptures.

Animals draw upon their instincts in order to function in the various cycles of their lives; for example, preparing for winter, nesting, mating, and raising young. As humans, we, too, have an inner knowledge that can be drawn upon to sustain us through the cycles of our lives. People of ancient cultures drew upon this knowledge intuitively as well as through their rituals, folklore, and myths. Through disuse, we modern folk have lost both our intuitive and our mythological access to this primal knowledge. Through the study of Scripture and myth, we reawaken this lost knowledge. Through the practice of prayer and meditation, we regain access to this wisdom of the soul.

The biblical story of Exodus lies within the collective memory of the Judeo-Christian culture. As such, it is more than a historical account of a certain tribe of people: it is a story that still lives within each of us. Historically, it is the story of a tribe of Hebraic people escaping from a life of slavery in the land of Egypt, crossing the arid wilderness of the Sinai Peninsula, and arriving, eventually, in the Land of Canaan—the Promised Land. The significance of this story lies not just in the geographic escape from Egypt to Canaan but in what took place during the journey. It was not in the Promised Land but in the wilderness that the Israelites made the transition from a nomadic tribe of refugees to a nation with an identity, a covenant, and a mission.

Thus we discover the first lesson of this great story: the transforming power of the transition process lies not in our arrival at a certain destination but in our *experience* of the process itself. A transition is a journey. In our high-tech-instant-everything culture, we have forgotten the art of journeying. We travel much but rarely do we journey. When traveling, we mechanically relocate from one place to another. We climb into our plane, train, or automobile, and then we seek to be comfortable and to keep our mind busy until we arrive at our destination. When journeying, however, the journey itself is as important as the arrival at a destination. We are so changed by the journey itself that we arrive a different person than we were when we departed. And so it is with the transition process.

As we consider the Exodus story, we are concerned not so much with its historical accuracy as we are with the teaching it has for us. We will interpret the historical account primarily from a metaphysical perspective, focusing on those archetypes that are universal to the transition process. From this viewpoint, we see the story as a lesson; it teaches us as a dream teaches us—through symbolism. We see each person, place, and thing in this story as part of ourselves, as an archetypal symbol within the unconscious. Thus the story reveals its wisdom to us.[2]

The story begins with the Israelites living as slaves in the land of Egypt; they are in bondage to their Egyptian overlords. But it didn't begin that way. The Israelites originally settled in Egypt in response to a crisis about 400 years earlier: "There was famine in all lands; but in all the land of Egypt there was bread" (Gen. 41:54).

When Jacob learned that there was grain in

Egypt, he said to his sons, "I have heard that there is grain in Egypt; go down and buy grain for us there, that we may live, and not die" (Gen. 42:2).

Unbeknownst to Jacob, his son Joseph was living in Egypt and was in charge of selling the grain: "All the earth came to Egypt to Joseph to buy grain, because the famine was severe over all the earth" (Gen. 41:57). When Joseph's brothers arrived in Egypt, they did not recognize him, but eventually Joseph revealed his identity to his brothers and had them bring their father Jacob (also known as "Israel") down to Egypt to live: "Thus Israel dwelt … in the land of Goshen;[3] and they gained possessions in it, and were fruitful and multiplied exceedingly" (Gen. 47:27).

Initially, Egypt was a godsend—literally, a lifesaver. Yet, what saves us at one point in our history can later imprison us. Four hundred years after Jacob and his family settled in Egypt the circumstances changed significantly:

> "Now there arose a new king over Egypt, who did not know Joseph. And he said to his people, 'Behold, the people of Israel are too many and too mighty for us. Come, let us deal shrewdly with them, lest they multiply, and, if war befall us, they join our enemies and fight against us and escape from the land.' Therefore they set taskmasters over them to afflict them with heavy bur-

dens.... They made the people of Israel
serve with rigor, and made their lives bitter with hard service."
—Exodus 1:8-11, 13-14

Much of our old way of life, and indeed much
of our identity itself, was formed as a response to
some need that once existed. As children, we
adapted ourselves to the needs and desires of our
family in order to get our own needs met. We
formed beliefs, attitudes, and behavior patterns
that may have served us well in our childhood.
Thirty or forty years later, however, these same patterns may enslave us and make our life bitter
because the circumstances of our life are vastly different. The patterns of thinking, feeling, and
behavior that once existed to serve and to protect
us may now keep us in bondage. The Israelites'
bondage in Egypt is symbolic of this condition of
becoming a "prisoner of our past."

The escape from Egypt was initiated and led
by a man named Moses. (More correctly, we
could say that it was done by the Lord working
through Moses.) So let's look at the story of this
man's life.

We begin with Pharaoh, the king of Egypt, who
lived "in dread of the people of Israel." (This is
thought to be Rameses II who reigned in the thir-
teenth century B.C.E.)[4] Not only did Pharaoh
make "their lives bitter with hard service" but he
ordered the Hebrew midwives to put to death any

male child born of a Hebrew woman. The midwives secretly refused to carry out this order so the king "commanded all his people, 'Every son that is born to the Hebrews you shall cast into the Nile' " (Ex. 1:22).

When Moses was born, his Hebrew mother kept him hidden for three months. She then enclosed him in a basket of woven rushes sealed with pitch and concealed him among the reeds at the river's edge. Pharaoh's daughter came to bathe at this spot, and when she saw the basket, she sent a maid to fetch it. Upon opening it, the baby began to cry and the princess felt pity, realizing that it was one of the Hebrew children her father had ordered killed. Moses' sister Miriam had been posted a little distance away to watch. She approached the princess and offered to find a Hebrew nurse to suckle the child. This was agreed, and she ran off to fetch Moses' mother who then became his nursemaid! When he was older, the Pharaoh's daughter adopted him and gave him the name Moses. (From the Hebrew verb *Mosheh* meaning "to draw out.")

Moses' birth story follows the motif of the "divine child" archetype found in many stories. The model for this particular story was the much older legend of the great Mesopotamian king Sargon of Akkad.[5]

Metaphysically, the birth of the divine child is the birth of the fresh, innocent, creative expression of the "real Self" of each of us. June Singer describes how this child always brings the promise of a new life:

> The archetype of the divine child tends to appear in advance of a transformation in the psyche. His appearance recalls the marking of aeons in the history of the world which were heralded by the appearance of an infant who overthrows an old order and, with passion and inspiration, begins a new one.[6]

This new life, though potentially very powerful, is also fragile at its onset. The "Pharaoh" within us seeks to destroy it, for indeed, it threatens the old order of our life. It is necessary to carefully protect this new life by hiding it from the hostile forces of the old order. (Sometimes "Pharaoh" appears externally in the form of well-meaning friends or family members seeking to return us to "our old self.")

As a boy, Moses grew up in the royal court but remained aware of his Hebrew origin. Several years later, as a grown man, he saw an Egyptian flogging a Hebrew slave. Enraged by what he saw, Moses killed the Egyptian at a time when he thought no one would see him; he then buried the body in the sand. But he later discovered that he had been seen and that the deed was reported to Pharaoh, who then sought to kill him. Moses fled to the east into the Sinai Desert and stayed in the land of Midian.

Moses had some strong feelings about the conditions he saw in Egypt. He acted on those feelings and was then forced to leave Egypt because the deed he tried to hide had been discovered. We, too, may feel strongly about something and, out of fear, try to suppress those feelings—to "bury them in the sand." But a primary law of consciousness is: That which is hidden will some day be revealed. Denial of our true feelings may seem to work for a while, but the day comes when they can be hidden no longer and must be fully acknowledged. This may precipitate some form of transition for us, as it did for Moses.

In the wilderness of Midian, Moses refers to himself as a "stranger in a strange land" (Ex. 2:22 KJV), a sentiment shared by many people in the transition process! Eventually he came to work for a man named Reuel and married his daughter Zipporah. Tending Reuel's flocks one day, Moses came to the mountain of Horeb (or Sinai). He turned aside to examine a strange sight: a bush burning without being consumed. The Lord's voice came out of the bush commanding him to remove his shoes, for he was on holy ground. Moses was told that he had been chosen to lead his brethren out of their oppression and bring them to the Promised Land. Moses shrank from the task: "Who am I that I should go to Pharaoh, and bring the sons of Israel out of Egypt?" To reassure him, the Lord said, "I will be with you" and, at Moses' request, revealed His name: "I am who I am" (Ex. 3:11-12, 14). An exact translation of the name of the Lord cannot be given; "I am who I am" is but one of many possible translations. "I am that I am" is the most famous. The essential meaning of this name is that the Lord is that which is the foundation of all being, the first cause of all that exists.

For Moses, this experience was a "new beginning"; he was being called to a new identity and a new phase of his life. It is interesting that Moses responded by saying "Who am I that I should go to Pharaoh?" and that the Lord answered by saying "I will be with you" and then told Moses His name. The implication for all of us in the transition process is that the Lord is with us throughout. The name and nature of the Lord calls us to recognize the Presence in the midst of our challenge. We walk on holy ground!

The essence of who we are is this I AM; this transpersonal Self that cannot be defined or described by word or concept. The poet Kahlil Gibran writes of this: "For self is a sea boundless and measureless."[7] Moses, who was identified with his personal self, felt inadequate to the task. When we are identified solely with the personal self, the ego, we feel inadequate to the task of transformation. As we cultivate our awareness of the I AM and learn to surrender to this transpersonal Self (as Moses eventually did), we realize that our only limitations are those that are self-imposed.

At the direction of the Lord, Moses confronted

Pharaoh by saying: "Thus says the Lord, the God of Israel, 'Let my people go'" (Ex. 5:1). Pharaoh flatly refused and even denied any awareness of the Lord. Only after suffering through ten terrible plagues did Pharaoh finally agree to let the Israelites go.

Now let's look at Pharaoh. To the Egyptians, Pharaoh was much more than a king; he was a deity, the embodiment of the divine. Metaphysically, in this account, Egypt symbolizes the unawakened life, the life governed by an external reality. Pharaoh is the ruler of this world; he symbolizes the personal ego, the self separated from an awareness of the Lord of our being. He rules with the ever-present fear that stems from the sense of separation from our true nature. Often, it's only after we are plagued by great suffering that we are willing to surrender to the voice of the Lord speaking to us. Only after suffering immense hardship—including the death of his own son— did Pharaoh agree to let the Israelites go ... and even then he changed his mind!

> "When the king of Egypt was told that the people had fled, the mind of Pharaoh and his servants was changed toward the people, and they said, 'What is this we have done, that we have let Israel go from serving us?' So he made ready his chariot and took his army with him, and took six hundred picked chariots .... The

Egyptians pursued them, all Pharaoh's horses and chariots and his horsemen and his army, and overtook them en-camped at the sea."

—Exodus 14:5-7,9

The old reality is not easily forgotten, and just when we think that we have "put the past in the past," lo and behold, it's chasing us in force! At times it's easy to become fearful and discouraged, as did the Israelites.

"When Pharaoh drew near, the people of Israel lifted up their eyes, and behold, the Egyptians were marching after them; and they were in great fear. And the people of Israel cried out to the Lord; and they said to Moses, 'Is it because there are no graves in Egypt that you have taken us away to die in the wilderness? What have you done to us, in bringing us out of Egypt?' "

—Exodus 14:10-11

Caught between the Egyptian army and the Red Sea, there appeared to be little hope left for the Israelites.

Caught between memories of a past now gone and an uncertain future, we may feel anxiety and regret, for we might appear to be in a hopeless sit-uation. We may lament our previous decisions:

"For it would have been better for us to serve the Egyptians than to die in the wilderness" (Ex. 14:12).

The solution to this dilemma is clearly given in the story itself:

> "And Moses said to the people, 'Fear not, stand firm, and see the salvation of the Lord, which he will work for you today; for the Egyptians whom you see today, you shall never see again. The Lord will fight for you, and you have only to be still.' The Lord said to Moses, 'Why do you cry to me? Tell the people of Israel to go forward. Lift up your rod, and stretch out your hand over the sea and divide it, that the people of Israel may go on dry ground through the sea.' "
>
> —Exodus 14:13-16

The rest is history: Moses lifts his rod, the Red Sea parts, and the Children of Israel cross the parted sea. The Egyptians pursue only to find the sea returning to engulf them; all the Egyptians drown, and the Children of Israel are free to pursue their destiny.

This is a very powerful lesson in letting go of the past and stepping forward into our life. The teaching consists of two parts: first, stand firm in knowing that the Lord, the I AM of your being, will work for you today—be still and know; and the second part is to step forward in faith and courage.

The lifted rod is a symbol of power, not worldly power, but the power of Spirit working through you as you call it forth. This power can work seeming miracles in your life. Don't cry to the Lord for help, but rather claim the creative power of God already at work in your life ... and then move forward in faith, despite all apparent obstacles.

The exodus from Egypt was an ending. The Exodus story is an archetypal portrayal of endings. Rich in symbolism, this story is a veritable gold mine of practical Truth. We saw that Egypt was not inherently a bad place ... in fact at one time in Israel's history, it was a very good place—it saved them from disaster. But the children of Israel outgrew their environment. We, too, may outgrow our circumstances—good though they once were—and we, too, need an internal Moses to lead us beyond our old life. Like the children of Israel, we may murmur and complain, we may feel fear and anxiety, we may cling to the past ... but always the Lord of our being is there, leading us, guiding us, calling us forward to freedom.

Chapter Summary

1. We humans inherit collective memory patterns known as "archetypes." These are not personal memories but belong to the entire human race.

2. These archetypal memories can be discovered through the study of dreams, myths, and ancient Scriptures, and also through the practice of prayer and meditation.

3. The biblical story of the Exodus lies within the collective memory of our culture; as such, it is more than just history, it is a story that lives within each of us.

4. The first lesson we learn from this story is that the transforming power of the transition process lies not in our arrival at some destination but in our experience of the process itself.

5. The Exodus story reveals its lessons through its symbolism.

6. The Israelites were slaves to the Egyptians. Originally they settled in Egypt in response to a crisis in their land. (See Gen. 41:54-57; 42:1-5.)

7. What saves at one point in our journey can later imprison us. (See Ex. 1:8-14.) As children, we formed certain patterns of thinking, feeling, and behaving in order to get our needs met; as adults, these same patterns might keep us in bondage.

8. The leader of the Exodus was a man named Moses. The story of Moses' birth follows the motif of the "divine child" archetype. This represents the fresh, innocent, creative expression of the true Self. The

"Pharaoh" within us (the ego) seeks to destroy this new life. (See Ex. 1:1-22; 2:1-10.)

9. Out of anger, Moses killed an Egyptian and tried to bury the body. He discovered that he had been seen and was forced to flee Egypt. We, too, may try to "bury the past," but ultimately "all secrets will be discovered." When this happens, it may precipitate a transition for us as well.

10. The Lord ("I am that I am") appeared to Moses and told him that he was to lead his people out of Egypt to the Promised Land. Moses eventually (and very reluctantly) agreed. (See Ex. 3:1-22; 4:1-17.) It is the Lord of our being who leads us out of our bondage; if we are identified with the personal self (as was Moses) we, too, may feel inadequate to the task.

11. Egypt represents the unawakened life ruled by external conditions. Pharaoh, who was the ruler of this world represents the personal ego. As with Pharaoh, often it is only after we are plagued with great suffering that the ego relinquishes control and we can hear the voice of the Lord (I AM). (See Exodus, Chapters 5-12.)

12. Pharaoh changed his mind and pursued the Children of Israel. The old reality is not easily forgotten; just when we think we've finally let go—here it comes again! Caught between memories of a past now gone and an uncertain future, we may feel anxiety and regret. (See Ex. 14:1-12.)

13. The solution is given in the story. (See Ex. 14:13-16.) This is a very powerful lesson; it consists of two parts: First, stand firm in knowing that the Lord (I AM) will work for you today, and then, step forward in faith and courage.

14. The Exodus story is an archetypal portrayal of endings. Like the Children of Israel, we, too, may outgrow our circumstances, and we, too, need an internal Moses to lead us out of our old life. Always, the Lord is there, guiding us forward toward freedom.

The Void

6

"You say I am repeating
Something I have said before. I shall say it
      again.
Shall I say it again? In order to arrive there,
To arrive where you are, to get from where
      you are not,
    You must go by a way wherein there is no
        ecstasy.
In order to arrive at what you do not know
    You must go by a way which is the way of
        ignorance.
In order to possess what you do not possess
    You must go by the way of dispossession.
In order to arrive at what you are not
    You must go through the way in which you
        are not.
And what you do not know is the only thing
      you know
And what you own is what you do not own
And where you are is where you are not."
                                    —T. S. Eliot[1]

In the Ending stage, we are preoccupied with

"what once was but is no more." At such times we may struggle with a myriad of feelings: fear, anger, confusion, perhaps guilt or remorse, and eventually, grief. Endings are often tumultuous times, sometimes likened to an earthquake. The Void, by contrast, is empty, flat, void of anything that seems solid or definite. If an Ending could be likened to an earthquake, then the Void could be likened to being lost in the desert or adrift on an endless sea. In the Void, time and space seem to lose their former reality; self seems like a phantom—a ghost from a former incarnation; life feels flat and empty, nothing seems quite real. Every attempt to "snap out of it" or to "pull oneself together" ultimately proves futile; it's like trying to put "Humpty Dumpty" together again.

The Void touches our deepest fears of helplessness, of abandonment, of death. Indeed, most of us would do *anything* to avoid these feelings. It is the avoidance of these feelings that is behind many of our addictive and dysfunctional behavior patterns. These behaviors are defenses, but in the Void, it seems there is little desire to defend. Consequently, we may feel vulnerable, and in some sense, we *are* vulnerable because our former ego defenses have fallen away.

With the ego boundaries weakened or missing, the unconscious may invade consciousness with strange and unfamiliar feelings, thoughts, and images. "This isn't me!" is a common response to these alien intruders. Sometimes the "visitors" may appear in the form of negative or even demonic feelings, desires, and images; conversely, we may encounter very positive and very powerful images or feelings—sometimes to the extent of appearing supernatural in origin.

In the traditional rites of passage, it is in the Void, in the "nonworld" between worlds, that the initiate encounters the transpersonal Self. This could appear in the form of a power animal, a spirit guide, a medicine symbol. Through contact with this higher Self, the initiate is imbued with new powers which will ultimately serve the entire tribe. Before he receives this power, however, he must face the "demons" within himself, the dark repressed aspects of consciousness that must be encountered and overcome. He is challenged to draw upon his deepest resources in order to survive this ordeal.

We, too, may feel challenged to draw upon our deepest resources during times of transition. Difficult as this time may be, it can be an enormously powerful period: a time of opening to new freedom and empowerment, a time of deep healing, a time of transformation. To gain the full benefit of this time, it is necessary to appreciate the need for this phase of our life experience, to see it within the context of a larger vision that sees beyond the limitations of the former self.

In the Void, without the familiar forms and structures, our life may feel barren and empty. Yet this can be a wonderful opportunity to view our life—and our self—from a new perspective. In times of barrenness, we may be able to see that which was previously hidden from our view. One time, during my own experience of the Void, I was walking through the woods on a winter day when I noticed how stark and barren was the naked forest standing amidst the snow-covered earth. There was a quiet sadness present in the woods, a sense of emptiness. Yet I was struck by the unique beauty of the winter forest and by the fact that I could now see much farther and more clearly than I could amidst the summer's lushness. I then realized that in this "winter" of my life, this time of emptiness, I had the opportunity to see more clearly that which was hidden from my former view. In the emptiness, we are given to see that which is not visible to eyes veiled with familiar surroundings.

Just as there are seasons of nature changing one to another, so there are seasons of the soul as it journeys through time and space. As every winter is followed by spring, so every death is followed by rebirth, every sorrow followed by joy, every Void followed by a New Beginning.

Kahlil Gibran writes:

> And could you keep your heart in wonder at the daily miracles of your life, your pain would not seem less wondrous than your joy;
> And you would accept the seasons of

your heart, even as you have always accepted the seasons that pass over your
fields.[2]

Each season of our life is to be honored. These
times can teach us much if we will listen. Yet we in
the West have a fear of the season of emptiness: we
don't trust it; we try to fill it with something or
seek to find a distraction. Culturally, we tend to
see growth as an additive process, an ever-expanding movement into more and more ... and more.
Rarely do we think of growth in terms of letting
go, yet letting go is an essential step in re-creation;
it is a vital part of any creative process. In the biblical creation story, "The earth was without form
and void, and darkness was upon the face of the
deep" (Gen. 1:2). Creation begins with emptiness.
It is from emptiness that new life emerges.

The new self is born from this emptiness and
darkness. In her book *Woman and Nature,* Susan
Griffin writes:

> If we allow the night, if we allow what
> she is in the darkness to be, this knowl-
> edge, this that we have not yet named:
> what we are. Oh, this knowledge of what
> we are is becoming clear.[3]

The Void can be seen as a time when we shed
the husk of our old identity—the false self we've
been conditioned to believe is "me"—and become

more clear about who we really are. It can be a death of the old mortal self and a rebirth into the eternal Self. Wu Ming Fu, a Chinese poet and philosopher, writes:

> The seed that is to grow
>   must lose itself as seed;
> And they that creep
>   may graduate through
> chrysalis to wings.
>
> Wilt thou then, O mortal,
>   cling to husks which
>   falsely seem to you
>   the self?[4]

In many Eastern philosophies, the Void is seen as the underlying reality behind the phenomenal universe. Buddhist meditation teachers often refer to "sacred emptiness" as the state of knowing one's true nature. Taoist teachings emphasize emptying oneself in order to experience the Tao, the ultimate reality. Lao Tsu, author of the *Tao Te Ching*, writes: "In the pursuit of learning, every day something is acquired. In the pursuit of Tao, every day something is dropped."[5]

Certain Western mystics have also taught the value of emptying oneself and entering into a state of nothingness. The thirteenth-century German mystic, Meister Eckhart, writes, "God is not found in the soul by adding anything, but by a process of subtraction."[6] And Saint John of the Cross, a sixteenth-century Spanish mystic, writes:

> To reach satisfaction in all
>   desire its possession in nothing.
> To come to possess all
>   desire the possession of nothing.
> To arrive at being all
>   desire to be nothing.
> To come to the knowledge of all
>   desire the knowledge of nothing.[7]

In order to become who we really are, we must let go of who we are not. In letting go of who we are not, we enter into the experience of nothingness, of nonbeing. In allowing ourself to have the experience of nonbeing, we come more fully into our true being. The Void is a passageway to becoming truly alive and fully awake. As Lao Tsu has written, "To die but not to perish is to be eternally present."[8] In a time of personal transition, during a period of deep emptiness, I wrote the following:

> Emptying ...
>   Sinking ever deeper
>   Into the darkness ... into the Void;
> Formless ...
>   Stripped of all flesh ...
>   Standing naked in the emptiness of
>   nonbeing;
> Ever deeper ...

Into the nothingness ... beyond form ...
Beyond the formless;
No movement ... no desire ... no sound ...
Pure silence ... beyond silence ...
Beyond death ...
To Life: the Origin ... the Source;
To Re-Creation!

Very often individuals in transition will ask: "What should I do while in the Void? What practical steps can I take to help me through this process?" We will devote the remainder of this chapter to addressing these questions.

• To make a general statement: In the Void, the way out is the way in; the quickest way through the Void is to embrace each experience fully ... and then let it go. That which we resist will persist. Enter fully into each feeling and each experience, but try not to get lost in any of it.

• If possible, avoid making any major decisions or long-term commitments in this period. At this time, our emotions are so volatile and our perspectives so changeable that we might find that the "person" who made the decision might not be the same person who will have to live with it!

• Don't try to "push the river." Don't attempt to rush your process or force anything to happen. Accept each day as it comes. Don't try to reconstruct the past or to go back to the old way of life; it probably wouldn't work if you tried!

• Pray and meditate for regular periods each

day.

• Trust in God. Trust in your own inner Wisdom. Trust, even when you feel hopeless!

• Take care of yourself physically. These may be stressful times. Eat wholesome meals; exercise regularly; get plenty of rest.

• Pay attention to your dreams. This may be a time of vivid or unusual dreams. Keep a dream journal.

• Keep a daily journal. Record your primary thoughts, feelings, insights, and experiences each day.

• Develop a support system.* This could include a counselor, friends, family, and/or a support group. Have someone with whom you can share your innermost thoughts and feelings. Choose someone with whom you feel safe.

• Create some type of ritual to symbolize your passage from the old life to the new. This could be done alone or with trusted friends. Express your feelings creatively, this could be through poetry, art, music, dance, song. Find ways to express your deepest feelings—whatever they may be.

*See Appendix for ideas about forming a "transitions support group."

Chapter Summary

1. An Ending is often a time of turmoil and confusion; the Void is a time of emptiness and flatness.

2. In the Void, time and space seem to lose their reality, self seems like a phantom.

3. The Void touches our deepest fears; most would do anything to avoid these feelings.

4. In the Void, the unconscious may invade consciousness with very strange feelings and images.

5. In the rites of passage, it is in the Void that the initiate encounters his transpersonal power, but first he must face the dark side of himself. He is challenged to the fullest.

6. This can be a difficult period of life but a very important one—an opportunity for new freedom and empowerment, a time for transformation.

7. Just as there are seasons of nature, there are seasons of the soul—periods when something "dies" and is reborn.

8. Each season is to be honored; we can learn much from each of them. Yet we in the West have a fear of the season of emptiness; we seek to avoid it.

9. All creation begins with emptiness. It is from the emptiness that new life emerges. The new self is born from the emptiness.

10. The Void can be seen as a time when we shed the

husks of the old self to become more of who we really are.

11. Many mystics—both Eastern and Western—emphasize the importance of "sacred emptiness."

12. The Void can be seen as a passageway to becoming truly alive and fully awake.

13. There are several practical things that one can do to aid the journey through the Void. (See Appendix.)

Wandering
in the Wilderness

7

Returning now to the Children of Israel: we find them safe from harm, having narrowly escaped the Pharaoh and his men who were drowned when the parted Red Sea returned upon them.

> "Thus the Lord saved Israel that day from the hand of the Egyptians; and Israel saw the Egyptians dead upon the seashore. And Israel saw the great work which the Lord did against the Egyptians, and the people feared the Lord; and they believed in the Lord and in his servant Moses."
>
> —Exodus 14:30-31

Once the celebration of having survived "Pharaoh and his gang" had ended, the Israelites were confronted with the harsh reality of their present situation: they were in the desert without food or water; they had no idea where they were going; and they were virtually defenseless against any hostile force that they might encounter.

Furthermore, the Israelites, having lived many generations under the rule of the Egyptians, were unfamiliar with the nomadic life of the desert. Moses was the only one with any "desert training," which he had received from his own journey into the wilderness. But Moses had another invaluable resource: direct access to the Lord, which proved many times to be the only thing that saved the Children of Israel.

Let's relate those events to our own wilderness experience. In the Ending stage, we are preoccupied with the past—with the "Egyptians" that are chasing us! Eventually, the Egyptians "drown" as we fully accept the experience of the Ending and the past is no longer our primary focus. This is both good news and bad news! The good news is that we are now ready for the next step in our transition process. The bad news is that the next step is often a tough one! We now step into the wilderness, the Void, and we may feel lost and vulnerable, as did the Children of Israel. Yet we have a "Moses" within us—one who has had "wilderness training." This internal Moses has direct access to the Lord of our being—the I AM within each of us. Like the Children of Israel, we often find that this is the *only* thing that saves us.

In the desert, the most critical need is for water. The first water the Israelites discovered was in the wilderness of Shur at a place called Marah, but they could not drink the water because it was bitter. The people murmured against Moses (the first of several "murmurs"), quickly forgetting the "vote of confidence" they had given him three days earlier!

The Lord then showed Moses a tree and directed him to throw it into the water, and the water became sweet! The Lord then made a covenant with the Children of Israel:

> "If you will diligently hearken to the voice of the Lord your God, and do that which is right in his eyes, and give heed to his commandments and keep all his statutes, I will put none of the diseases upon you which I put upon the Egyptians; for I am the Lord, your healer."
>
> —Exodus 15:26

We see here a pattern which is repeated many times during the wilderness experience: the people experience a crisis, they murmur against Moses, the Lord intervenes and saves them, and then a covenant (a promise) is made by the Lord to the people of Israel. Sometimes this covenant is an unconditional promise and sometimes the promise is conditional—the condition usually being obedience to the Lord.

This covenant has relevance to our own transition process. The Lord symbolizes the I AM within each of us: our divine essence. If we listen to the voice of this inner Lord—the "still small voice" of our intuition—and follow the guidance we receive, we will be immune to the "dis-eases" of the ego (the Egyptians). Indeed, this Lord within is our healer: it is this power that brings us to wholeness. When we listen to and follow this inner voice, we become free of the many maladies that plague the ego-centered consciousness.

In the Void, when all the normal "rules" have vanished, this inner voice may be all that we have to guide us. And we eventually find that this voice is infinitely more reliable than all the rules that we once used as our guide. And yet the Israelites symbolize a part of ourselves as well, and like them, it may take us a while to learn to heed this inner voice.

The Israelites continued their journey without incident into the wilderness of Sinai until the fifteenth day of the second month in the desert. Then another crisis arose: there was no food! The people again murmured against Moses: "Would that we had died by the hand of the Lord in the land of Egypt, when we sat by the fleshpots and ate bread to the full; for you have brought us out into this wilderness to kill this whole assembly with hunger" (Ex. 16:3).

The Lord responded to the people's need: "Behold, I will rain bread from heaven for you; and the people shall go out and gather a day's portion every day, that I may prove them, whether they will walk in my law or not....

"At twilight you shall eat flesh, and in the morning you shall be filled with bread" (Ex. 16:4, 12).

That evening several quail came into the camp. The people quickly caught and ate them. In the morning a dew covered the ground. When the dew evaporated, there remained a strange substance, which proved to be edible. This was the "bread from heaven" that was promised them. This "manna" would appear every day, except for the Sabbath, for the next forty years. Although none would appear on the Sabbath, twice the usual amount would appear on the preceding day. And strangely, the manna would spoil if not consumed within the same day, except for the extra amount that was provided for the Sabbath!

The Lord guided the Children of Israel through the wilderness with a pillar of cloud by day and a pillar of fire by night. They were confronted with many trials and dangers, and yet each challenge was met with a "miracle" of the Lord. One time they were about to die of thirst when water began to flow from a rock struck by Moses. At another time, a fierce tribe known as Amalekites attacked them. Against all odds, the battle was won ... but only as Moses would keep his hands raised!

In the uncertainty of the Void, we are tempted to look back to former times when things seemed more secure. The freedom of the wilderness can lose its appeal when our needs go unmet, and we may regret the loss of the once familiar bondage. Yet we discover that our needs *are* met in new and sometimes unexpected ways if we listen to and follow the voice of the Lord within.

We may receive guidance in some unusual and surprising ways as well—and often when least expected. For example, we may open a book at random and discover there just the answer that we need or a casual conversation with someone might suddenly reveal the insight that guides our next step. We may even see our answer appear in such unlikely places as bumper stickers or billboards or hear it in the words of a popular song! If we ask and listen, we will be guided ... somehow. It is essential that we not only listen to, but also obey the direction of the inner Lord, for we *will* be led along our right path.

In the third month of their journey, they came into the wilderness of Sinai. The Lord called Moses up Mount Sinai and told him to take this message to the Children of Israel: "If you will obey my voice and keep my covenant, you shall be my own possession among all peoples; for all the earth is mine, and you shall be to me a kingdom of priests and a holy nation" (Ex. 19:5-6).

The Lord told Moses that he would descend from the mountain in three days to speak to him in the sight of the people. After three days a thick cloud covered the mountain; lightning and thunder and then the blast of a trumpet came from within the cloud. The whole mountain quaked, and the people trembled in fear. The Lord called Moses to the top of Mount Sinai and dictated to him the Ten Commandments and a variety of other laws governing the people's worship practices and their daily lives. The Lord then promised victory to the Children of Israel over the inhabitants of Canaan, and He also warned them not to worship the gods of the Canaanites.

When Moses descended, he built an altar at the foot of the mountain and feasted with the tribal elders. Then the Lord called him back up the mountain to give him the Commandments written on stone tablets. This time the Lord gave Moses detailed instructions as to the building of a tent sanctuary whose innermost chambers would house the tablets upon which the Commandments were recorded. Moses was up on the mountain with the Lord for forty days. Meanwhile, down below, the people grew restless; they were afraid that Moses had disappeared forever. Desperate for spiritual leadership, they melted down their gold jewelry and fashioned it into a golden calf, which they began to worship amidst a wild revelry. When Moses finally returned and saw what was happening, he was enraged. He threw down the tablets of stone and broke them into many pieces; he melted down the golden calf, and when it cooled, the gold was ground into dust and was mixed with water that he forced the people to drink!

Eventually the people repented, and the Lord again wrote the Commandments in tablets of stone which Moses had cut. The people then constructed the holy tabernacle and the Ark of the Covenant according to the directions dictated to

Moses. The Ark of the Covenant, which contained the stone tablets, was placed within the tabernacle. The construction was completed and then "the cloud covered the tent of meeting, and the glory of the Lord filled the tabernacle....

"Throughout all their journeys, whenever the cloud was taken up from over the tabernacle, the people of Israel would go onward; but if the cloud was not taken up, then they did not go onward till the day that it was taken up. For throughout all their journeys the cloud of the Lord was upon the tabernacle by day, and fire was in it by night, in the sight of all the house of Israel" (Ex. 40:34, 36-38).

At this point in Israel's history, its people were transformed from a tribe of wandering nomads to a nation with an identity, a covenant, and a mission. The covenant at Sinai was a landmark event: it ordained Israel as the Lord's "chosen" and a "holy people" and a "nation of priests."

One might say that this was Israel's experience of initiation. Like most initiations, it wasn't easy. The Israelites experienced doubt, fear, confusion, regression, and finally, repentance. Initiation takes place in the Void, often occurring at deep levels of the psyche—unknown to the conscious mind. Here the seeds of rebirth are sown.

Not yet ready for fruition, a struggle ensues between the new consciousness and the old. We may vacillate, filled with faith and promise one day only to find ourselves worshiping the "golden calf" of the past on the next. We worship this golden calf when the "old mind" gains control, when we regress into negative and self-defeating thinking, feeling, and behavior patterns created in the past.

"I thought I had worked through that one!" is a common statement—usually spoken with great chagrin. We find that this "golden calf" must be "melted down, ground to powder, and swallowed." The old must be released, but we must learn the lesson of each experience before we completely let it go. It cannot be released until it is melted down and consumed in our consciousness: it must be transmuted and assimilated through awareness, acceptance, and forgiveness.

Whatever regressions or setbacks we may seem to be experiencing, it is very important that we continue to do our inner work and to have faith. What appears to be regression is a normal part of any evolutionary process. Eventually we *will* regain our conscious connection to the Lord within, and we *will* be guided every step along the way.

The Lord now dwelt among the people and was clearly guiding them along the route they were to follow. The Lord led them into the wilderness of Paran—very close to the borders of Canaan, the Promised Land. Under instructions from the Lord, Moses sent twelve spies into Canaan to scout the land and report back to the people of Israel. A man named Joshua, assisted by a young man named Caleb, led the scouting party. They were gone for forty days.

When they returned, Joshua and Caleb gave their report:

> "We came to the land to which you sent us; it flows with milk and honey .... Yet the people who dwell in the land are strong, and the cities are fortified and very large"(Num. 13:27-28).

But the other spies were much more pessimistic, and they spread fear among the people:

> "The land ... is a land that devours its inhabitants; and all the people that we saw in it are men of great stature.... And we seemed to ourselves like grasshoppers, and so we seemed to them" (Num 13:32-33).

The people were filled with fear, and they murmured against Moses. Many of them wanted to return to Egypt. Moses pleaded with the people to trust in the Lord, but to no avail. The Lord was angry! After repeatedly fulfilling His promises, the people still would not trust. So the Lord decreed:

> "Of all your number, numbered from twenty years old and upward, who have murmured against me, not one shall come into the land where I swore that I

would make you dwell, except Caleb ...
and Joshua .... And your children shall be
shepherds in the wilderness forty years,
and shall suffer for your faithlessness,
until the last of your dead bodies lies in
the wilderness" (Num. 14:29, 33).

The thought of wandering forty years in the
wilderness was more than many of them could
bear. A band of Israelites decided to take matters
into its own hands. Despite warnings from Moses,
the people took up arms and marched into
Canaan. Without Moses, without the Ark of the
Covenant, without the Lord leading them, they
entered into the land of Canaan ... and they were
quickly defeated. Many died that day at the hands
of the Amalekites and the Canaanites.

None who left Egypt as adults would live in the
Promised Land, except for Joshua and Caleb. For
the next forty years, the people of Israel wandered
in the wilderness.

Finally, after seemingly endless hardships and
setbacks, the Children of Israel once again came
within sight of the land of Canaan. All the people
who had murmured against the Lord had died
and were buried in the wilderness. The old generation had died, a new generation had been born.
By now, Moses was a very old man ... his remaining
days were few in number.

Moses gathered together the new generation of
the Children of Israel and taught them the laws of

God, and he blessed each of the tribes. Moses then turned leadership of the young nation over to Joshua, who would eventually lead them into the Promised Land. The Lord called Moses up the mountain of Nebo from which he could view the Promised Land. Moses saw the Promised Land, but he would not live to set foot upon it.

At the age of one hundred twenty years, Moses died. The people of Israel wept for their beloved leader. He was to be revered forever by their descendants. The closing verses of the book of Deuteronomy pay tribute to this great man: "And there has not arisen a prophet since in Israel like Moses, whom the Lord knew face to face" (Deut. 34:10).

The Children of Israel were at the threshold of the Promised Land but were not yet ready to enter. It would be a whole new generation of Israelites that would march into the Promised Land. Even Moses, their leader, would not enter this place.

If taken literally, this might seem very unfair, yet this illustrates an important principle: In the process of transformation, nothing happens before its time. Divine order is at work in our transition process; an essential element of this order is timing.

It is not uncommon within the Void that we encounter the opportunity for what appears to be a new beginning. Our personal self may desperately long for something to happen and yet it doesn't. We may be tempted to take matters into our own hands and try to force the issue, but like the Children of Israel, this only delays our progress and may create even more suffering.

The Israelites were required to wander for forty years. The number *forty* in the Bible generally refers to "a period of time needed to prepare for something." It is not always to be taken in a literal sense.

Quite simply, the Israelites needed more time to prepare themselves before entering the Promised Land. The old generation had to die out; a new generation had to come into being. This is why we may have to wait longer than we sometimes like. Internally, within the deeper parts of the psyche, changes are taking place—changes that we may not be aware of. An old generation of consciousness must die, and a new generation of consciousness must be born. This takes a certain period of time. How long? Symbolically, forty years. Literally speaking, the only answer to that question is that it takes as long as it takes.

There has been much discussion among Bible students and scholars as to why Moses was not allowed to enter the Promised Land. The clearest answer is that it simply was not his job. His function was to take the Israelites out of the bondage of Egypt, lead them through the wilderness, and take them *to* the Promised Land. The name *Moses* means "to draw out," and that is exactly what he did. Moses symbolizes that part of our consciousness that leads us out of the old life, guides us through the Void, and takes us to (but not into) the New Beginning.

Chapter Summary

1. Having escaped from Pharaoh, the Israelites are now confronted with life in the wilderness, with little in the way of provisions or experience. Their most important resource was Moses' access to the Lord. (See Ex. 14:30-31.)

2. In the Ending stage, we are preoccupied with the past. Eventually the past is no longer our primary focus, and we move into the next phase of the process: the Void. Here we may feel lost and vulnerable; however, we have direct access to the Lord of our being—the I AM.

3. The Israelites encounter water that is not fit to drink until the Lord intervenes with a miracle; the Lord then makes a covenant with the Israelites. (See Ex. 15:22-26.)

4. In the Void, our usual guidelines for living have vanished; we may have only the internal voice of the I AM to guide us. Ultimately, this is all that we need.

5. The Israelites encounter another crisis: there is no food! The Lord intervenes, providing manna and quail. The Lord continues to guide and to protect the Children of Israel, often in some very unusual ways. (See Exodus, Chapters 16-17.)

6. The Lord calls Moses up Mt. Sinai to deliver another covenant—one that includes the Ten Commandments. While Moses is away, the people forsake the Lord and worship a golden calf. When Moses returns, he is enraged, and he breaks the tablets of stone. Eventually the people repent, and new tablets are created. (See Exodus, Chapters 19-40.)

7. Israel's initiation took place in the wilderness; our initiation takes place in the Void. It is not an easy process; we may struggle and regress as we vacillate between the old life and the new. This is a natural part of the evolutionary process; gradually, the new life takes root.

8. The Israelites were led close to the land of Canaan. Joshua, Caleb, and others scouted the new land. Some of the spies brought back very discouraging reports. The people were fearful and murmured against Moses. In anger, the Lord decreed that no one over the age of twenty (except Joshua and Caleb) would live to see the Promised Land; they were destined to wander in the wilderness another forty years. (See Numbers, Chapters 13-14.)

9. After forty years of wandering, the Israelites returned to the edge of the Promised Land. The old generation had died. Moses was a very old man. He blessed all the tribes and turned leadership over to Joshua. Moses died without entering the Promised Land. (See Deut. 31:14-30; Chapters 32-34.)

10. In the Void, we may encounter what appears to be a new beginning before we are yet ready. If we try to force the matter, it leads only to more suffering. An "old generation" of consciousness must die before we are ready for the next step.

11. Moses had served his purpose, which was to lead the Israelites out of Egypt, guide them through the wilderness, and take them to the threshold of the Promised Land. It was not his function to take them into the new land; this task was to be given to Joshua, the new leader.

New Beginnings:
The Promised Land?

8

"I learned this, at least, by my experiment: that if one advances confidently in the direction of his dreams, and endeavors to live the life which he has imagined, he will meet with a success unexpected in common hours. He will put some things behind, will pass an invisible boundary; new, universal, and more liberal laws will begin to establish themselves around and within him; or the old laws be expanded, and interpreted in his favor in a more liberal sense, and he will live with the license of a higher order of beings."

—Henry D. Thoreau[1]

Having experienced the Ending and the Void, we are finally ready for the New Beginning. We may tend to think of a New Beginning in terms of an external change, but it actually begins as an internal experience. It may be experienced as a subtle inner shift: a new sense of readiness, an inner awakening. Sometimes our dreams presage the New Beginning. Dreams of birth, of moving into a new house, of discovering something new are often signals that a new life is emerging.

On the other hand, we may not be aware of the New Beginning until there is an external change in our life. The internal signals may be so subtle that our conscious awareness fails to recognize them. Then we are awakened to the New Beginning by a shift in our outer world—perhaps a sudden and unexpected shift. The external change may occur even before we feel ready; we might feel inadequate or unprepared for the opportunity before us.

When a New Beginning occurs, the external circumstances of our life reflect the internal transformation that has already taken place. In the traditional rites of passage, the initiate receives new powers from his encounter with transpersonal forces and then returns to the tribe in a new way, prepared to use this new power to serve the greater good. In the New Beginning, we, too, "return" empowered with wisdom and strength gained from our encounter with the transpersonal Self—the I AM within. This encounter takes place during the wilderness experience—in the emptiness of the Void. We, too, will use this new power to benefit our world, whatever "our world" may be. We find that this new wisdom and power are not given to us solely for our own benefit but are given that we may serve others in some way.

The external New Beginning may occur before or after we feel ready for it; it may be expected or unexpected. And yet, as we pray for guidance and divine order, trusting in God at work in our life, the New Beginning will occur at exactly the right time and in the right way. And we will be equal to any task that life brings to us, for we are never given a challenge beyond our ability to master it.

One of the best ways to prepare for a New Beginning is to discover your soul's deepest desire. A true New Beginning will be some expression of this desire. And how do we discover our soul's desire? This is an extremely personal endeavor, so it is difficult to give a "formula" answer. Yet there are some questions that you can ask yourself in order to facilitate this discovery:

What is it that I have always enjoyed doing?

What has always come naturally for me?

What have I felt naturally drawn or attracted to?

What would I do with my life if I were not concerned with money?

What would I do if I knew I could not fail?

If I were to die today, what would feel unfinished in my life?

What is it that is so important to me that I would risk everything in order to achieve or experience it?

And here is an exercise that you can do:

Imagine that your whole life until now, including your identity itself, was simply a story that was written by someone else. Now you can write the rest of this story. You can design the rest of your life. And you can write your own identity. Who

113

would you be? What would your life be like? How would the story end?

A question that often arises around this topic is whether or not one should focus on specific results. One side of this debate says that the subconscious mind needs very specific images to work with in the manifestation process. The other side says that it is best not to be too specific because we may be limiting our good—God may have a better idea than we have.

Perhaps the best approach is to be specific about the nature and quality of the experience that we desire but not be too specific about the particular form that it should take. Our soul's desire is to express itself in some unique way. It is important for us to determine *what* it is that is seeking expression. Specifically *how* this is to occur can be left open to divine order.

In my own life, there was a time when I found it necessary to let go of all material attachments and to surrender everything to God's will. I waited only for God to tell me what to do. I waited several weeks for my "guidance" to come, only to hear nothing. Finally, in prayer one day, the answer came. The answer was in the form of a question: What do *you* want to do?

I became aware that my soul's deepest desire was to teach—to teach the spiritual truths that I had learned and continue to learn in my life experience. I wanted to teach through the media of seminars and lectures and also through writing and personal counseling. How this was to occur I had no idea, nor was I concerned. Having determined the essential nature of my desired experience, I let God determine the form and the timing.

Once I chose the general direction that I wanted to go and made the commitment to do whatever was needed to implement this choice, I felt a movement occur in my life. This movement was the first of a series of steps that led me to my current life experience. And my current experience does include teaching—through seminars and lectures—as well as writing and counseling. And indeed, God *did* have a better plan than I ever would have conceived.

Surrendering our personal will to the higher will does not always preclude the need to make our own choices. I believe that it was necessary for me to formulate my desires *and* surrender the results. It would seem that the process unfolds in a pattern of letting go and surrendering, making choices and commitments, and then letting go and surrendering once again. We are in a partnership with the divine: at times we must lead, and at times we must follow.

Sometimes we may attempt an external beginning before we are internally ready. We may feel uncomfortable in the Void and eager to "get on with our life," and through the power of our personal will acting alone, we may *make* something happen. What we've then created is not a New Beginning but a "pseudobeginning." A *pseudobegin-*

ning is not living a new life but is simply living the old life in a new form. An external change is not necessarily a New Beginning. For example: A person could divorce his or her spouse and marry another person and yet still have essentially the same relationship. We could say "It's the same dance ... with a different partner." A New Beginning is a new "dance", even if it's with the same partner!

The question may arise: How can I tell a true New Beginning from a pseudobeginning? You can examine your desire for the New Beginning. This desire may be what Ken Keyes, Jr., calls an "addiction" or it may be a "preference." Keyes defines an addiction as "an emotion-backed demand or desire for something you tell yourself you must have to be happy." A preference, on the other hand, is "a desire that does not make you upset or unhappy if it is not satisfied."[2]

If you are "addicted" to the New Beginning, then you should examine the addiction before you concern yourself with the New Beginning. If you are convinced that the New Beginning is going to make you happy, then guess again! If you are unhappy in the Void, then you will be unhappy in the New Beginning. Nothing outside of yourself can make you happy (or unhappy).

To repeat something we said in a previous chapter: the fastest way out of the Void is *through* it. We need to make peace with each present-moment experience. Each experience needs to be honored and to be seen as our teacher. Trying to "rush the process" ultimately results in more suffering.

A true New Beginning will occur only after we have completed the inner work that is part of the previous stages. And when we are internally ready, we will find a way to create the external beginning, or perhaps we could say that it will find us. There is a fascinating synchronicity between our inner and outer worlds! New Beginnings often occur in unexpected ways. An event that appears to be a mistake or even a breakdown may turn out to bring forth the external beginning. The best approach is to be ready, but not anxious; to be alert, but not willful. Continue to pray, to trust, and to know that your life *is* in divine order.

As with the other stages, a New Beginning brings its own set of challenges. It's a change, and remember, no matter how much we may consciously desire change, there is nearly always a part of ourselves that doesn't want to change. Sometimes we unconsciously resist the New Beginning. A New Beginning puts us in unfamiliar territory; we don't have much experience with this new way of life. We may feel unsure of ourselves, maybe somewhat awkward and vulnerable. Like Moses, we may have a fear of being unprepared or inadequate for the task at hand. This anxiety can show up in our dreams as scenarios of being called upon to perform in some way and then finding ourselves unprepared, late, or inadequately dressed!

A New Beginning will call forth the need for new commitments—not always an easy thing to do! A commitment challenges us to take concrete action—to "walk our talk." It requires discipline, and often sacrifice.

For example, a commitment to become a musician or an athlete means many hours of practice—practicing even when we don't want to. It means giving up the activities that we might otherwise be involved with at that time. A commitment to marry someone means giving up all other possibilities for marriage with someone else. It means honoring the marriage commitment even when you wished that you weren't married!

A true commitment is not an obligation to something or someone outside of yourself, but rather is a commitment to yourself. It is an agreement with yourself that you will give up some freedom in a certain area of your life in order to enrich other areas of your life, and in the long run, to generate even more freedom.

Making a commitment brings with it the possibility of failure. This could trigger any fears we have about failure. It may bring up some unhealed memories from the past. A commitment means being willing to risk oneself in order to invest in something that one believes in. To never face the fear of failure is to never make a commitment.

A commitment may touch our fear of rejection. Any time we take a stand for something, we find that someone may disagree with us. Making a commitment means being willing to stand in the face of criticism. We may find that some of our family, friends, or colleagues do not support our new commitments—and may even oppose them.

Given the potential hardships involved, we may be tempted to hold back from making new commitments, yet it is only through commitments that a true New Beginning will occur. A true commitment is a decision that puts very powerful forces in motion.

W. H. Murray was a mountain climber who led an expedition to the summit of Mount Everest—not something one does without a commitment! A poster I saw quoted him as saying:

> Until one is committed there is hesitance, the chance to draw back, always ineffectiveness. Concerning all acts of initiative, there is one elementary truth, the ignorance of which kills countless ideas and plans: that the moment one definitely commits oneself, then Providence moves too. All sorts of things occur to help one that would never otherwise have occurred. A whole stream of events issues from the decision, raising in one's favor all manner of unforeseen incidents and meetings and material assistance, which no man could have dreamt would have come his way.

To be committed is to accept responsibility for being a creator in one's life. It means being willing to be a cause rather than a reaction to the circumstances of one's life. No great thing has ever been accomplished without commitment.

And finally, let us note that not all New Beginnings result in dramatic changes in one's outer life. Sometimes a transition may involve a deep inner change and yet will return us to external circumstances not unlike those before. There is a familiar Zen saying:

Before enlightenment—all day: chop wood, carry water.

After enlightenment—all day: chop wood, carry water.

In the long run, we may find that very little has changed externally, but *internally*, we are no longer living in the same world. We may find ourselves involved in the same external activities, yet experiencing them in a totally new way. The poet T. S. Eliot captures the essence of this experience:

And the end of all our exploring
Will be to arrive where we started
And know the place for the first
    time.[3]

Returning one last time to our Bible story: we

find that after many fierce battles, the Children of Israel finally conquer the Promised Land. And we see that it was Joshua, not Moses, who led the conquest. Joshua was a military leader, a warrior, a man of action. This tells us that a new archetype within consciousness is required to lead us into the New Beginning. We must call upon the "inner warrior." It is this warrior that embodies the qualities of strength, courage, discipline— and commitment.

The word *Joshua* is the Hebrew version of the Greek word *Jesus*. This name is derived from the word *Jehovah*, meaning "I am that I am." *Joshua* is an expression of the "I AM," the Lord of our being. Jesus represents the fullest expression of the "I AM."[4]

Historically, both Joshua and Jesus were leaders, taking their followers into new territory: Joshua in a physical sense, Jesus in a spiritual sense. Both Joshua and Jesus represent the consciousness of New Beginning, of New Life. Joshua leads us into the promised land of the New Beginning. Jesus leads us into the kingdom of heaven—the state of ever-expanding spiritual awareness. Jesus leads us to the "ultimate" New Beginning, which is the awareness that we are spiritual beings having a human experience, in truth, ever and always one with God—the Father within.

Chapter Summary

1. A New Beginning starts as an internal experience, often a very subtle one. We may detect the inner cues or we may not be aware of the New Beginning until there is an external change in our life.

2. When a New Beginning takes place, the external circumstances of our life begin to reflect the internal transformation that has already taken place.

3. As we pray for guidance and trust in God, we will experience the New Beginning at the right time and in a way that is right for us.

4. One way to prepare for a New Beginning is to discover your soul's deepest desire. There are some specific questions you may ask in order to facilitate the discovery process. (See page 113.)

5. How specific should we be in envisioning desired results? Perhaps it is best to specifically imagine the quality of the desired result without being too specific on the form that it should take.

6. It seems that we are in a partnership with God. At times we need to act and at other times just be still and listen.

7. Sometimes we may create an external beginning before we are internally ready. What we've then created is only a pseudobeginning—not the real thing.

8. How to tell a true New Beginning from a pseudobeginning? Examine your desire for the New Beginning. Is it an addiction or a preference?

9. If you are addicted to a New Beginning, then deal with the addiction itself before attempting the New Beginning.

10. A true New Beginning will occur only after we've completed the work from previous stages ... and when we are internally ready, we will somehow find a way to create the New Beginning.

11. A New Beginning brings its own set of challenges. We are often in unfamiliar territory; we may have a fear of being unprepared for our new task.

12. A New Beginning calls forth the need for new commitments. A commitment challenges us to concrete action and often to sacrifice.

13. A true commitment is not to anything outside of yourself but is actually a commitment to yourself. It is an agreement to sacrifice in some area of your life in order to enrich other areas of your life.

14. Making a commitment means risking failure or rejection. Unless we are willing to face our fear, we will never make a real commitment.

15. A true commitment puts very powerful forces in motion.

16. To be committed is to accept responsibility for being a creator in one's life. No great thing has ever been accomplished without commitment.

17. Not all New Beginnings involve dramatic external changes in our life. Perhaps very little has changed externally, but internally, we are no longer living in the same world. (Chop wood, carry water.)

18. Returning to the Bible story: The Children of Israel, under the leadership of Joshua, finally conquer the Promised Land. Joshua is a symbol of the warrior—an embodiment of the qualities of strength, discipline, and courage. These are all needed for a New Beginning.

19. The names *Joshua* and *Jesus* both represent expressions of the "I AM": the Spirit of God individualized in and as each of us.

Part
III

The
Plan Unfolds

"The sun went down on Tuesday.
It was a full day.
It dawned with all the fresh
    innocence
Of every new day.
It unfolded its morning
    with promise,
With plan,
With vision,
With dreams.
A full noon crowned its zenith.
Then almost imperceptibly,
The shadows began to lengthen ...
Not unpleasant, but welcome
Was the shade of the afternoon.
The plan had been revealed,
The vision cleared,
The dream became retrospect.
The sky began to spread the news
    that
The day was done.
The sun went down on Tuesday ...
Wednesday dawned with its own promise.

O God of all the days complete,
Help me to understand
The beginnings and the ends
So that I may let go the past
And, in so doing,
Go renewed and free
Into the new day
You plan for me."

—Dorothy Pierson[1]

In this world, all things change. Although change sometimes appears random and chaotic, not one thing in our life occurs without purpose—albeit the underlying purpose is rarely evident at first. Very often it's only in retrospect, after the passage of time and the healing of our pain, that we begin to perceive a purpose behind our life transitions.

Imagine a caterpillar crawling across an intricately designed Oriental carpet. This caterpillar sees nothing but an endless series of colors changing from one to another. Yet, a butterfly flying above the carpet can readily see the pattern underlying the caterpillar's journey. Indeed, there *is* a pattern, a plan, for each of us; although, most of us are like the caterpillar on the carpet, we see only a series of apparently unrelated events occurring before us.

Within the nucleus of each cell in our body exists a DNA molecule which directs the destiny of that cell. Likewise, within each soul, a divine plan guides the evolution of that soul. And within the collective soul of humanity, a divine plan is at work directing the path of our evolution.

Pierre Teilhard de Chardin, a Jesuit priest and a distinguished paleontologist, believed in such a plan. In his book *The Phenomenon of Man,* he articulates his vision of the physical universe as a dynamic manifestation of ever-evolving consciousness. In this system, humanity—as a species—is an essential link in the progressive unfoldment of consciousness from the most primal substance of the universe to the culmination of all evolution—the Omega point, conscious oneness with God.[2]

This evolution of consciousness is the driving force behind all physical evolution. According to Teilhard, the purpose of the physical universe is to serve as a vehicle for consciousness to develop. And in this scheme, the human—as a self-aware being—is evolution reflecting upon itself.

Evolution, according to Teilhard, occurs in stages. The development of consciousness occurs within each stage according to a pattern of increasing complexity. When a certain threshold of complexity is reached, a convergence takes place: a critical point at which evolution will "dead-end" or will make a quantum leap into an entirely new level of consciousness.

According to this theory, primal substance evolved into atoms and then into inorganic molecules and then into complex organic molecules, and then a quantum leap took place: Life was born! In parallel fashion, life slowly evolved from a single-celled organism to the complex creature known as a human, and then another quantum leap: Thought was born! Thinking evolved from the rudimentary thoughts of the ape-man to the genius of Shakespeare, Mozart, and Einstein.

Today our world is saturated with complex thoughts and massive amounts of information. In some areas of human inquiry, we may have reached the limits of our understanding. And some believe that we are on the threshold of a quantum leap into the next stage of our evolution.

What is this next stage, this stage "beyond thought"? Since the future is unknown, we can only guess; and even if we did know, we could not describe it because language itself is a product of thought. We can, at best, "point to it" with language, but we cannot explain it, and we cannot comprehend it with the intellect.

A Zen proverb says, "The finger that points to the moon is not the moon." The distance between our speculation about this next level of being and being in it is even greater than the distance from the finger pointing to the moon and the moon itself.

So how can we best "point to" this next level? One way to do this is to look at some individuals who appear to have already made this "quantum leap" to the next level of being.

A Buddhist legend tells of Siddhārtha Gautama (the Buddha) who became enlightened after a long sitting under the Bodhi tree. After his enlightenment, he was walking down a road when a man approached him and noticed his extraordinary countenance.

In awe of what he saw, he asked the Buddha, "Sir, are you a god?"

To which the Buddha replied, "No."

"Then are you a man?"

"No," the Buddha replied again.

"Well, what are you?"

The Buddha replied, "I am awake."

Five hundred years after the time of Buddha lived a teacher named Jesus of Nazareth (the Christ) who was also "awake." He preached a radical message: "The kingdom of heaven is at hand" (Mt 4:17). And he demonstrated his realization of this "kingdom" through the extraordinary life that he lived. He gave numerous metaphors and parables about the nature of this kingdom, and yet he was unable to describe it directly with words.

Perhaps we could label the next stage of evolution as "awakening" or as "entering the kingdom of heaven." Maybe it is futile to attempt to describe this next stage, yet we can address the very important question, "How do we get there?"

In Teilhard's model of evolution, we see that each movement upward from one level to the next is a major transition—a quantum leap. And we see that each quantum leap is preceded by some type

of crisis, by a severe strain upon the system as it
exists. This is also noted by Barbara Marx
Hubbard in her book *The Evolutionary Journey*. She
reflects upon fifteen billion years of evolution with
this insight:

> Crises precede transformation. Before
> every quantum change, "problems"
> emerge—limits to growth, stagnation,
> unmanageable complexity, impending
> catastrophes, disintegration. From the
> perspective of the present, the crises look
> like mistakes, deadly errors in the system.
> But from the perspective after the quan-
> tum transformation, these problems are
> seen to be "evolutionary drivers," vital
> stimulants which trigger astounding
> "design innovations."[3]

And what "design innovation" is about to take
place? Hubbard writes:

> Conscious evolution is the word we
> place on the evolutionary map. The inno-
> vation needed now is *to understand the
> magnificent processes that created us and pur-
> posefully cooperate with them in planning and
> designing our own future.* It is essential for
> survival.[4]

Thus we are being called upon to become partners in the cosmic dance! Evolution can no longer take place without us. We are not just the product of evolution, but we are now the architects of it.

And how do we go about becoming an "architect of evolution"? We each begin with our own life—our personal path of evolution. Our individual life is intrinsically connected with the evolution of all life on this planet. Richard Wilhelm writes in *The Secret of the Golden Flower:*

> The psyche and the cosmos are related
> to each other like inner and outer worlds.
> Therefore man participates by nature in
> all cosmic events, and is inwardly as well
> as outwardly interwoven with them.[5]

Crisis precedes transformation in the global scheme in the macrocosm, and so crisis precedes transformation in the life of the individual—in the microcosm. Crisis itself, however, does not automatically produce transformation. The crucial factor lies in the way we handle our crisis—our attitude toward it. Marilyn Ferguson writes in *The Aquarian Conspiracy:*

> At the level of ordinary consciousness,
> we deny pain and paradox. We doctor
> them with Valium, dull them with alcohol, or distract them with television....
> Our ability to block our experience is

an evolutionary dead end. Rather than experiencing and *transforming* pain, conflict, and fear, we often divert or dampen them with a kind of unwitting hypnosis....

Conflict, pain, tension, fear, paradox ... these are transformations trying to happen. Once we confront them, the transformative process begins.[6]

The key element in dealing effectively with crisis is that of a mindful awareness: a willingness to consciously experience our discomfort without denial or distraction. Awareness is essential for transformation. Ferguson goes on to say:

Anything that draws us into a mindful, watchful state has the power to transform .... Mind, in fact, is its own transformative vehicle, inherently prepared to shift into new dimensions if only we let it.[7]

Crisis precedes transformation, but not all crises lead to transformation. To be transformational, a crisis must be attended with an open-minded watchfulness.

One of the definitions of the word *crisis* is "a crucial turning point." The very word *crisis* is derived from a Greek word meaning "to decide." Sometimes our decisions are made automatically and unconsciously, the result of "old programs" operating in the subconscious mind. This may be especially true when responding to a crisis situation. Acting unconsciously, we are not responding to the circumstances of the present moment. We are actually responding to past circumstances. Through mindful self-observation, we can avoid this "evolutionary dead end" and make choices based on our inner wisdom operating in the present moment—new and creative choices that lead to growth and transformation.

A crisis is, by definition, a turning point in our life, yet through mindful awareness, we can often anticipate these turning points before they manifest themselves as major difficulties. As Lao Tsu has written:

> Because the sage always confronts
>   difficulties,
> He never experiences them.[8]

Each crisis can be a turning point that leads to the death of an old way of being and to the birth of new life. Indeed, evolution proceeds through a process of deaths and rebirths, of endings and new beginnings. Out of fear and ignorance, we often resist our endings, our deaths. Our human conditioning may lead us to believe that "all is lost forever." Yet wisdom and faith allow us to see beyond the appearance of tragedy, to the new life beyond. We then begin to see each ending, each death, not as a tragedy, but as a prelude to transformation.

In his book *Illusions,* Richard Bach writes:

> The mark
> of your ignorance is the depth
> of your belief in injustice
> and tragedy.
>   What the caterpillar
>   calls the end of the world,
>   the master calls a
>   butterfly.[9]

Some believe that humankind is now confronted with the need to draw upon unprecedented faith and wisdom in order to transcend our own humanness. Perhaps this is the only hope for our survival. Yet the leap into the unknown is frightening: an existential fear grips us. This collective angst is described vividly by Greek writer Nikos Kazantzakis:

> Blowing through heaven and earth, and in our hearts and the heart of every living thing, is a gigantic breath—a great Cry—which we call God. Plant life wished to continue its motionless sleep next to stagnant waters, but the Cry leaped up within it and violently shook its roots: "Away, let go of the earth, walk!" Had the tree been able to think and judge, it

would have cried, "I don't want to. What are you urging me to do! You are demanding the impossible!" But the Cry, without pity, kept shaking its roots and shouting, "Away, let go of the earth, walk!"

It shouted in this way for thousands of eons; and lo! as a result of desire and struggle, life escaped the motionless tree and was liberated.

Animals appeared—worms—making themselves at home in water and mud. "We're just fine here," they said. "We have peace and security; we're not budging!"

But the terrible Cry hammered itself pitilessly into their loins. "Leave the mud, stand up, give birth to your betters!"

"We don't want to! We can't!"

"You can't, but I can. Stand up!"

And lo! after thousands of eons, man emerged, trembling on his still unsolid legs.

The human being is a centaur; his equine hoofs are planted in the ground, but his body from breast to head is worked on and tormented by the merciless Cry. He has been fighting, again for thousands of eons, to draw himself, like a sword, out of his animalistic scabbard. He is also fighting—this is his new struggle—to draw himself out of his human scabbard. Man calls in despair, "Where can I go! I have reached the pinnacle, beyond is the abyss." And the Cry answers, "I am beyond. Stand up!"[10]

We are being called to go beyond ourselves as we now exist. Individually and collectively, we are being pushed to the limits of our humanness. Frightening though this may seem, each step along the way is guided by God—the "great Cry" within each of us. The divine plan is unfolding within and through each of us.

A question we often hear is, "What is the divine plan for my life?" The answer can rarely be stated in words, but it can be found by simply looking at what is in front of us. Step by step, day by day, the plan unfolds before our very eyes. The path we must take is the path we are on.

No one else can walk this path for us. Others can, at best, serve as guides. Stephen Levine writes, "Buddha left a road map, Jesus left a road map, Krishna left a road map, Rand McNally left a road map. But you still have to travel the road yourself."[11]

We have many inspired teachers and teachings to guide us, but the map is not the journey, the menu is not the meal, the finger pointing to the moon is not the moon.

The plan unfolds by means of "whatever it takes." This is how we got to where we are now, and this is how we will get to where we are going.

We are reminded of this in the following poem by
Martha Smock:

> Could we but see the pattern of our
>   days,
> We should discern how devious were
>   the ways
> By which we came to this, the present
>   time,
> This place in life; and we should see
>   the climb
> Our soul has made up through the
>   years.
>
> We should forget the hurts, the
>   wanderings, the fears,
> The wastelands of our life and know
> That we could come no other way or
>   grow
> Into our good without these steps our
>   feet
> Found hard to take, our faith found
>   hard to meet.
>
> The road of life winds on, and we like
>   travelers go
> From turn to turn until we come to
>   know
> The truth that life is endless and that
>   we
> Forever are inhabitants of all
>   eternity.[12]

There was no other way for us to arrive at this present point in our life's journey, and we will arrive at each destination by whatever it takes to get there.

Like the caterpillar on the carpet, we usually see only a small piece of the "big picture." Yet, unlike the caterpillar, we are not just passive observers in the events of our life. We are active participants in all events cosmic and mundane. We have within our soul the divine plan seeking fulfillment through each of us. We are evolution becoming conscious of itself.

> We have in our bodies, hearts, minds and spirits the wisdom of the ages. We have at our fingertips all the wonders of modern technology. We have the East and the West, the yin and the yang—infused, informed and guided by the brilliant intention of evolution. The time is here to envision and co-create the adventure of conscious evolution.
>
> —Barry McWaters[13]

Chapter Summary

1. Everything changes, and sometimes change seems chaotic. In spite of appearances, nothing occurs without purpose.

2. Imagine a caterpillar on an Oriental carpet. Most of us are like the caterpillar in that we don't see the "big picture."

3. Within each soul, a divine plan guides its destiny. Within the collective soul of humanity, a divine plan is at work.

4. Teilhard had a vision of the physical universe as a manifestation of evolving consciousness. He saw humanity as a vital link in the plan.

5. According to Teilhard, evolution occurs in long periods of slow change punctuated by quantum leaps from one level of consciousness to another. Some believe that today we are on the threshold of a quantum leap to the next level of evolution—beyond thought.

6. What is the next stage? We don't know, and even if we did, it would not be explainable. We can at best "point to it" with words.

7. One way to "point" is to look at those who have made the "quantum leap," such as Jesus and the Buddha. Perhaps it is futile to speculate on the nature of the next stage, but we can ask "How do we get there?"

8. In Teilhard's model, each quantum leap is preceded by a type of crisis.

9. Crises are evolutionary drivers which stimulate astounding design innovation. The innovation now needed is to understand and cooperate with the processes that create us. (See Hubbard quotes, p. 132.)

10. How to do this? We begin with our own life. We are intrinsically connected with the cosmos. Our personal crises are preludes to evolution.

11. Crisis does not automatically produce evolution; another factor is needed: a mindful awareness. (See Ferguson quotes, p. 133-134.)

12. The word *crisis* comes from a Greek word meaning "to decide." Through mindful self-observation, we can make new choices that lead to transformation.

13. A crisis is always a turning point, yet it doesn't have to be a catastrophe.

14. Each transformation is a death and a rebirth to new life. It may take faith to see this.

15. Humanity is being confronted with the need to transcend its own humanness. This is not easy, but it is necessary.

16. "What is the divine plan for my life?" That which is in front of us. We each have to walk our own path.

17. The plan unfolds by "whatever it takes." There is "no other way" for us to have gotten to where we are now.

18. We are not passive observers in the events of our life. We are cocreators, and the time is here to envision and cocreate the adventure of evolution.

Beyond Change?

"At the still point of the turning world.
     Neither flesh nor fleshless;
Neither from nor towards; at the still
     point, there the dance is,
But neither arrest nor movement. And
     do not call it fixity,
Where past and future are gathered.
     Neither movement from nor towards,
Neither ascent nor decline. Except for
     the point, the still point,
There would be no dance, and there is
     only the dance."

—T. S. Eliot[1]

Is it possible to find anything permanent in a world that is continuously changing? The desire for security and stability is a fundamental human drive. Out of this desire for security, we may attempt to cling to people, possessions, roles, and titles; but deep inside, most of us know that seeking security in the external world is like building a sand castle before the incoming tide: we're simply buying time against the inevitable. Everything that we see and touch will someday crumble to dust. And yet an inner voice tells us that there must be something that is changeless. Is there? And if so, how do we find it?

In our study of the transition process, we have encountered several paradoxes, such as "an ending is a beginning" or "to find ourselves, we must lose ourselves." In this chapter, we discover yet another paradox: By fully surrendering to the process of change, we discover that which never changes. By fully surrendering to the ever-changing reality of our world, we discover a changeless Reality beneath and beyond the phenomenal world.

Let's explore this idea. By fully surrendering to the process of change, we are referring to an attitude of surrendering to the natural flow of life. This attitude of surrender is sometimes referred to by other names, such as "nonresistance," "acceptance," "nonattachment," or "equanimity." This attitude, whatever called, refers to the way in which we meet the moment-by-moment experiences of our life.

To surrender fully is to be open, in a deep way, to each experience of our life. It means to allow ourselves to feel fully each response to the events and the circumstances of our life. It means to be totally oneself, to live fully in each moment. This requires letting go of our attachment to how we think we should be and to be unconditionally accepting of how we are right now. It requires a willingness to look at each part of ourselves as it arises moment-by-moment—denying nothing, condemning nothing.

Surrender, as we use the term here, is an internal experience. Being surrendered in this way does not mean becoming a "doormat" for others to walk upon. We can say and do what is necessary to protect and to assert ourselves in the world. Likewise, accepting each part of ourselves does not mean acting out every thought, feeling, or desire. We can behave in a sane and responsible way and still be fully surrendered internally. We do what we need to do in the world in a way that is appropriate for our well-being and for that of others, *and* we fully allow each internal experience to occur without interference—simply observing each thought, feeling, desire, memory, and physical sensation—and then letting go.

Interestingly, when we are fully surrendered in this way, we will naturally begin to behave in ways that are beneficial to ourselves and others. It is when we suppress and condemn parts of ourselves that these suppressed parts are acted out unconsciously in destructive ways. By being willing to experience all aspects of self, we are gaining more consciousness in all areas of our life.

Being surrendered means that we don't try to control and orchestrate the flow of our life; we let life unfold. Yes, we ask for what we want; we voice our opinion when appropriate; and we act when we need to act—but we are not attached to the results. We become less concerned with the external content of our life, less concerned with the past and the future, and more concerned with how we are living our life in each moment. We begin to see that the true quality of our life is not dependent upon external circumstances.

Let's talk more about what this experience of surrender is *not*. It is not "giving up" or "quitting." It is not resignation or despair. Surrender is a conscious "giving over" of oneself to something greater. To use an analogy, one might say that a skillful canoeist must "surrender" to the river; likewise, an expert sailor has learned to "surrender" to the wind. Surrender is not abdicating responsibility for the way we live our life. It is living responsibly and skillfully by allowing a greater reality to direct the course of our life.

To explore this idea further, let's look at the opposite of surrender: resistance. Resistance is refusing to accept our present moment experience. Resistance occurs in the body primarily as tension and rigidity. It occurs in the mind in a variety of ways, such as judgment, anger, and fear. It may also appear in more subtle forms such as rationalization, confusion, or denial. Some type of resistance is at the core of all compulsive and addictive behaviors.

At yet a deeper level, we see that clinging to an outmoded identity or self-image can be a way of resisting the natural flow of life. Our self-image is primarily the product of our conditioning. From the moment of our birth (if not before), we are subjected to the promptings and expectations of our family and culture. They tell us (often nonverbally) who we are ... and, at that time, we have little choice but to believe them. But if we continue to cling to this "programming" from the past, we may be resisting the fullness of life as it seeks to express through us right now.

Most of our resistance is unconscious. Simply willing oneself to surrender is rarely enough to overcome this deeper resistance. It is necessary to be mindful of each moment-by-moment experience so that the subtle resistances can be consciously seen and released. Continuous practice of mindful awareness combined with an attitude of nonjudgmental acceptance will eventually dissolve all resistance in consciousness.

Our conditioned response to virtually every unpleasant experience is to "tighten up and turn away." It takes insight and perseverance to retrain oneself to "open up and allow" each experience to occur as it naturally seeks to happen.

As we consciously observe ourselves—observing our thoughts, feelings, words, and behaviors—we begin to see the deeper places within ourselves where we are holding, refusing to let go, refusing to surrender. Continued observation shows us that this holding is the cause of much suffering. Resistance to any painful experience will ultimately cause more suffering than the original pain itself. With this insight, we begin to let go, to surrender, at ever-deeper levels.

Stephen Levine, a teacher of meditation, writes:

> If you are trying to be someone doing something, controlling the flow, then when that which is uncontrollable approaches, your resistance becomes greater and your suffering more intense. As you let go of control, you see ... "acceptance is magic."[2]

Indeed, we do discover that "acceptance is magic." Surrendering to the flow of life, the divine plan, we eventually find a new sense of peace and a new source of power. We experience the dance of life unfolding with less grasping and attachment ... and less suffering. Gradually, we begin to see that we are not living our life, but rather that our life is being lived through us. Life then takes on a flow, a rhythm, a synchronicity. With little effort, much is accomplished. Some would describe this as "living in the Tao" for in the *Tao Te Ching* it is written:

> The Tao of heaven does not strive,
>   and yet it overcomes.
> It does not speak, and yet is answered.
> It does not ask,
>   yet is supplied with all its needs.
> It seems at ease,
>   and yet it follows a plan.[3]

Inherent within this process of ever-deepening acceptance is a profound trust in the innate wisdom and goodness of the natural process of evolution, the divine plan, the Tao. The breadth and the depth of this natural wisdom and goodness cannot be fathomed by the human mind; it can only be realized through experience. As Stephen Levine tells us, "When you let go of control of the universe, when you let go of everything, only the truth remains."[4]

In India there lived a man who embodied the essence of this principle; his name was Mahatma Gandhi. He freed his homeland from two centuries of foreign rule without firing a shot. Perhaps even greater than his political accomplishment was the spiritual legacy that he left to all of humankind. He demonstrated the incredible power that works through one who has deeply surrendered his life to the divine plan.

The principle Gandhi used he termed *satyagraha*. This is derived from the Sanskrit words *satya* which means "Truth" (literally: "that which is") and *agraha* which means "holding firmly." Gandhi called it "soul-force." Truth itself is a very real and powerful force when one holds to it without compromise. However, this holding must not be an activity of the personal self. Self-will blocks the release of soul-force; removing self-will frees it. One must surrender to the power of Truth.

In Gandhi's words, "There comes a time when an individual becomes irresistible and his action becomes all-pervasive in its effects. This comes when he reduces himself to zero."[5]

To do this requires one to have a radical trust in God at work in his or her life. As we embrace this trust, we find that the very force that shook our world and caused it to collapse around us— the force that we at first resisted, then gradually accepted, and now align with—was the very force that brought us home to our true Self. We are reminded of the man who said, "I prayed to God when the foundations of my life were being shaken ... only to find that it was God that was shaking them!"

So we begin to trust the "shakings," and we no longer resist the force that crumbles the structures of our life. What we once called a tragedy, we now see as an opportunity for greater freedom, wisdom, and power—not to be feared, but actually welcomed.

We begin to see everything in our life and in the universe as part of a great cosmic dance: the dance of life, evolving, unfolding, expressing Itself through us and around us. Gradually, our perception shifts; what once seemed so real and solid no longer appears that way: time and space become elastic; the world of form becomes transparent. A Hindu mystic would tell us that we have met Shiva Nataraj, the Cosmic Dancer, the god of creation and destruction, who sustains through his dance the endless rhythm of the universe.

And within this dance is the still point "where

past and future are gathered." At the still point, eternity exists within each passing moment; infinity exists within each dancing atom; the changeless exists in the heart of change itself. "Except for the point, the still point, there would be no dance, and there is only the dance."

We are both the dancer and the dance, the seeker and the sought, the knower and the known. What we have been looking for is that which is looking. We've come home to our Self.

But this is not the end ... it is only the beginning, for the dance goes on!

Chapter Summary

1. We may ask, "Is there anything permanent in this ever-changing world? And if there is, how do we find it?"

2. We find yet another paradox: By fully surrendering to the process of change, we discover that which never changes.

3. The term *surrender* refers to the way in which we meet the moment-by-moment experiences of our life.

4. To surrender fully is to be open, in a deep way, to each experience in our life—denying nothing, condemning nothing.

5. Surrender is an internal experience. We can be fully surrendered internally and yet function in the external world in a sane and responsible way.

6. Being surrendered means that we act as necessary, yet we are not attached to results; we don't try to control the flow of our life.

7. Surrender is not "giving up in despair"; it is simply allowing a greater Reality to direct our life.

8. Resistance is the opposite of surrender; it is refusing to accept our present experience. It can appear in many forms: tension, judgment, denial, or clinging to an outmoded identity. Most resistance is unconscious; it is necessary to practice mindfulness in each moment in order to dissolve all resistance within us.

9. Our conditioned response to unpleasant experiences is to "tighten up and turn away"; it takes insight and

perseverance to "open up and allow" each experience to occur naturally.

10. Recognizing that resistance causes more suffering; we let go at ever-deeper levels.

11. We see that "acceptance is magic." We experience our life being lived through us—with less attachment and less suffering. We live "in the flow of life."

12. Mahatma Gandhi exemplified the power that can flow through one who is deeply surrendered to Truth.

13. Surrendered, we live with a deep trust in the inherent wisdom and goodness of life. We trust even those forces that seem to "shake our foundations."

14. And we begin to see our life as part of the great cosmic dance—the dance of life, evolving and unfolding around and within us.

15. Within this dance, we can find the "still point" where eternity exists within each moment. The changeless exists within the heart of change itself.

Epilogue

From the Hasidic tradition comes this story of Rabbi Eisik, son of Rabbi Yekel in Cracow.

Eisik was a very pious man—and a very poor man. He was so poor that he lived in a one-room house with only a dirt floor. One night he dreamed that he was in the great city of Prague, many miles away. In the dream, he walked throughout the streets of the city admiring the beautiful buildings. Eventually he came to the edge of the city where he saw a bridge, and beyond the bridge a great palace. He walked across the bridge and began to dig, whereupon he discovered a buried chest. He opened the chest, and it was filled with gold, diamonds, and treasures of every sort!

When this dream was repeated for the third time, Eisik was convinced that it was a sign from God. He grabbed a shovel and began the long journey to Prague. After many days of walking, he was very tired and his feet were sore. Finally, he reached the city. Although he had never been in this city before, he recognized many of the buildings from his dream. And sure enough, he discovered the bridge, and beyond it, the palace. He crossed the bridge and began to dig. Soon his shovel struck something! It was the buried chest! With trembling hands and pounding heart, he opened the chest ... and it was empty!

Brokenhearted as never before, Eisik began to weep—and then to sob uncontrollably. Suddenly, he felt a hand upon his shoulder; it was a young man wearing the suit of a palace guard. "What happened old man? Why are you crying?" Eisik recounted his story. Upon hearing the tale, the young man laughed with scorn. "You are a foolish old man to put such faith in dreams—dreams are nonsense. I myself have many foolish dreams, and I pay no heed to any of them. Why, just last night I had a dream about a poor rabbi who was digging a hole in the middle of the dirt floor of his home, and there he found a buried chest—filled with treasure! Now, doesn't that show you how foolish dreams can be?"

Immediately, Eisik was on his feet. With renewed energy, he commenced the long journey back home. And there he discovered the priceless treasure buried within the place where he had lived in poverty most of his life.[1]

Appendix
Starting a Life Transitions Support Group

Group Objectives:

1. To provide safety and support for individuals experiencing the challenges of transition:
   a. By providing a safe place to share one's feelings.
   b. By providing the support of other individuals who are in (or have been in) the process of transition.
2. To provide teachings and resource materials that support one's spiritual growth and transformation within the transition process.

Group Functioning:

1. The group can function with a single permanent leader or with a rotating leadership. If the leadership rotates, one person is designated as the "facilitator" for each meeting.
2. The facilitator is responsible for:
   a. Opening and closing the meeting on time.
   b. Communicating any group guidelines (see #4 below).
   c. Ensuring that the guidelines are followed.
   d. Bringing some relevant material to read, listen to, or discuss with the group. This could include a book, magazine article, cassette tape, or simply a topic for discussion.

e. Performing duties such as turning out lights, locking up, collecting donations (if appropriate).

3. The meeting can begin with prayer if this is appropriate to the group. The facilitator shares group guidelines and any relevant administrative items. The meeting then proceeds with each member "checking in."

4. Suggested guidelines for checking in:

   a. Each person shares his or her present feelings and/or relevant experiences since the last meeting. (Note: sharing should be about one's own feelings and experiences; gossip, blame, and criticism of others are to be discouraged).

   b. All other members of the group listen to the person sharing.

   c. When the individual has finished sharing, others may respond with supportive comments; however, advice-giving, rescuing, and "fixing" are discouraged.

   d. The attitude toward each group member should always be one of caring and respect, yet always allowing the person to be responsible for his/her own feelings.

   e. Anyone who wishes not to share may simply say "I pass."

5. After "check-in," the facilitator then presents the material for discussion.

6. Before the meeting ends, any "business items" should be taken care of and a facilitator should be

designated for the next meeting (if necessary).
7. End with prayer and/or hugs if appropriate.

Notes

Prologue

1. Walt Whitman, "Song of the Open Road," Sections 9, 11, 13, *Leaves of Grass*, The New American Library, New York and Toronto, 1958, pp. 140-142.

Chapter 1, "The Paradox of Change"

1. Princeton Language Institute Staff, *Twenty-First Century Dictionary of Quotations*, Dell Publishing Co., Inc., 1993.
2. Another example: In the world of science, it was long assumed that the physical world is an objective reality existing independent of our observations. This seems to "make sense" because that is the paradigm that governs the way we see things. However, as Fred Allen Wolf explains, in the field of quantum physics, a paradigm shift has taken place. This is the recognition that everything that is observed is affected by the observer. There is no "fixed reality" independent of the observer; we change everything we see simply by the act of observing it. Some go so far as to say that the observer "creates" that which is seen by the very act of looking for it! See Wolf, *Taking the Quantum Leap*, Harper & Row, New York, 1981, p. 127.
3. Viktor E. Frankl, *Man's Search for Meaning*, Washington Square Press, Inc., New York, 1969, p. 154.
4. Ibid., p. 164.

Chapter 2, "The Process of Transition"

1. Holistic health has grown into a large, hard-to-define field. Essentially based on the idea that body, mind, and soul are intricately linked and that balance is required for health, its true origins go back to the beginnings of humanity's religions. Modern day medical pioneers like Kenneth R. Pelletier, O. Carl Simonton, and C. Norman Shealy were

among the first to espouse it. Humanistic psychology, like its younger sister *transpersonal psychology*, is usually attributed to the work of Abraham Maslow who pioneered the radical idea of studying healthy people to see what made them well rather than studying sick people to see what made them sick. The works of Carl Jung, Carl R. Rogers, Rollo May as well as Ken Wilber, Frances Vaughan, Roger Walsh, Stanislav Grof, and others are making this a powerful alternative to traditional psychology (Freudian and behavioral). Creation spirituality is the work of ex-Dominican priest Matthew Fox and is based on the idea that creation is inherently whole and good rather than separate and evil.

Chapter 3, "Rites of Passage"

1. Jean Houston, *The Search for the Beloved,* Jeremy P. Tarcher, Inc., Los Angeles, 1987, p. 106.
2. Kahlil Gibran, *The Prophet,* Alfred A. Knopf, New York, 1992, p. 52.
3. William Bridges identifies these as: Endings, The Neutral Zone, and The New Beginning. See Bridges, *Transitions,* Addison-Wesley Publishing Company, Reading, Mass., 1990, p. 88.
4. Joseph Campbell, *The Hero With a Thousand Faces,* Princeton University Press, 1968, p. 30.

Chapter 4, "Endings"

1. T. S. Eliot, "Four Quartets," *The Complete Poems and Plays,* Harcourt, Brace and Company, New York, 1952, p. 144.
2. Bridges, p. 92.
3. Alla Bozarth-Campbell, *Life Is Goodbye/Life Is Hello,* CompCare Publishers, Minneapolis, 1983, p. 25.
4. Stephen Levine, *A Gradual Awakening,* Anchor Books, New York, 1989, p. 39.
5. Bozarth-Campbell, p. 25.
6. Some other common enchantments of our culture:
    —If I work hard, I will succeed.

—If I succeed, everyone will like me.

—If everyone likes me, I will be happy.

—If I please others, I will get what I need.

—If I find the right husband, wife, job, school, house, and so forth, I will be happy.

7. William James, *The Varieties of Religious Experiences*, Macmillan Publishing Company, New York, 1961, p. 133.

8. Bridges, p. 102.

9. Murray Stein, *In Midlife*, Spring Publishing, Inc., Dallas, 1988, p. 22.

Chapter 5, "Departure From Egypt"

1. For a definitive description of the collective unconscious, see C. G. Jung, "Instinct and the Unconscious" and "The Concept of the Collective Unconscious," *The Portable Jung*, The Viking Press, New York, 1975, pp. 50-69.

2. One of the characteristics of the wisdom of the archetypal symbol is that its meaning is open-ended: there is no fixed or final meaning to a given symbol or story. Each symbol is organic, dynamic, alive; its meaning to us expands and deepens as we grow in consciousness.

3. Goshen was a land in Northern Egypt near the Nile delta.

4. Bernard W. Anderson, *Understanding the Old Testament*, Prentice-Hall, Inc., Englewood Cliffs, N. J., 1975, p. 42.

5. Ibid., p. 49.

6. June Singer, "The Motif of the Divine Child," in Jeremiah Abrams (ed.), *Reclaiming the Inner Child*, Jeremy P. Tarcher, Inc., Los Angeles, 1990, p. 49.

7. Gibran, p. 54.

Chapter 6, "The Void"

1. Eliot, p. 127.

2. Gibran, p. 52.

3. Susan Griffin, *Woman and Nature: The Roaring Inside Her*, Harper Colophon Books, New York, 1980, p. 168.

4. Wu Ming Fu, "Patterns in Jade," in Dorothy Berkley

Phillips (ed.), *The Choice Is Always Ours,* Harper San Francisco, 1989, p. 42.
5. Lao Tsu, *Tao Te Ching,* Translation by Gia-fu Feng and Jane English, Vintage Books, New York, 1989, verse 48.
6. Matthew Fox (ed.), *Meditations With Meister Eckhart,* Bear & Co., Santa Fe, N. Mex., 1983, p. 45.
7. Kieran Kavanaugh, *John of the Cross: Selected Writings,* Paulist Press, New York, 1987, p. 78.
8. Lao Tsu, verse 33.

Chapter 8, "New Beginnings: The Promised Land?"

1. Henry D. Thoreau, *Walden,* Dodd, Mead & Company, New York, 1946, p. 284.
2. Ken Keyes, Jr., *How to Enjoy Your Life in Spite of It All,* Living Love Publications, St. Mary, Ky., 1980, pp. 4-6.
3. Eliot, p. 145.
4. *Metaphysical Bible Dictionary,* Unity School of Christianity, Unity Village, Mo., 1931, p. 368.

Chapter 9, "The Plan Unfolds"

1. Dorothy Pierson, "The Sun Went Down on Tuesday," *Daily Word,* March 1981, pp. 4-5.
2. Pierre Teilhard de Chardin, *The Phenomenon of Man,* HarperCollins, New York, 1975.
3. Barbara Marx Hubbard, *The Evolutionary Journey,* Evolutionary Press, San Francisco, 1982, p. 27.
4. Ibid., p. 55.
5. Richard Wilhelm, *The Secret of the Golden Flower,* Routledge & Kegan Paul Ltd., London, 1950, p. 11.
6. Marilyn Ferguson, *The Aquarian Conspiracy,* J. P. Tarcher, Inc., Los Angeles, 1980, pp.74-76.
7. Ibid., p. 69.
8. Lao Tsu, verse 63.
9. Richard Bach, *Illusions,* Delacorte Press, 1977, p. 134.
10. Nikos Kazantzakis, "Report to Greco," in Dorothy Berkley Phillips (ed.), *Choice Is Always Ours,* p. 32.

11. Stephen Levine, *Who Dies?*, Anchor Books, Garden City, New York, 1982, p. 18.
12. Martha Smock, "Progress," *Daily Word*, Dec. 1947, p. 6.
13. Barry McWaters, *Conscious Evolution*, New Age Press, Black Mtn., N.C., 1981, p. 177.

Chapter 10, "Beyond Change?"

1. Eliot, p. 119.
2. Levine, pp. 189-190.
3. Lao Tsu, verse 73.
4. Levine, p. 194.
5. Eknath Easwaran, *Gandhi the Man*, Nilgiri Press, Tomales, Ca., 1978, p. 152.

Epilogue

1. This story has appeared in many places and in many forms; some texts credit Martin Buber with the first publication of this story. See Buber, *Tales of the Hasidim: The Later Masters*, Schocken Books, New York, 1948, pp. 245-246.

About the Author

Robert Brumet is chairman of pastoral studies at Unity School for Religious Studies at Unity Village, Missouri.

Brumet teaches courses in pastoral counseling, meditation, and world religions. He also conducts seminars and programs on a wide variety of topics related to spiritual growth. He has presented his programs at churches and retreat centers throughout North America. His lectures, seminars, radio broadcasts, and magazine articles have impacted the lives of thousands of people. His audiocassette *Life Transitions: Growing Through Change* and a series of articles in *Unity Magazine* have been precursors to the publication of this book.

Robert was ordained a Unity minister in 1980 and has served Unity churches in Evansville, Indiana, and Overland Park, Kansas. Before entering the ministry, he was a director of systems analysis for a Michigan manufacturing firm and an adjunct professor at two colleges in Western Michigan. A native of Toledo, Ohio, he received B.S. and M.S. degrees from the University of Toledo.

In his leisure time, Robert enjoys tennis, canoeing, bridge, writing, and meditating. He has four grown children and four grandchildren. He resides in Kansas City, Missouri.

Printed in the U.S.A.   50-4578-1M-6-03